the conscious cook

the conscious cook

Delicious MEATLESS recipes *that* will CHANGE the WAY you EAT

TAL RONNEN

Edited by Danielle Claro
Photographs by Linda Long

Designed by a|c air-conditioned

Produced by MELCHER MEDIA

Published by William Morrow *An Imprint of* HarperCollins *Publishers*

HarperCollins books may be purchased for educational, business, or sales
promotional use. For information, please write: Special Markets Department,
HarperCollins Publishers, 10 East 53rd Street, New York, NY 10022.

FIRST EDITION

Library of Congress Cataloging-in-Publication Data is available upon request.

09 10 11 12 13   10 9 8 7 6 5 4 3 2 1

ISBN: 978-0-06-187433-8

Printed in China

In loving memory of my grandfather Irving S. Norry, my sister Keren Ronnen Rosenberg, and my dear friend Angelo Favarolo

table *of* contents

kathy freston

Kathy Freston is the author of *Quantum Wellness:*
A Practical and Spiritual Guide to Health and Happiness

I first heard about Tal Ronnen from a friend. She couldn't stop raving about this gifted vegan chef who could win anyone over to a plant-based diet because his food was so divine. Tal, my friend told me, was on a mission to teach other chefs and restaurateurs how to cook well without meat so that vegetarian options might be more appealing, even to those who normally opted for meat. I remember thinking how great that was, and how it was perfect for the times since there was a growing number of people who wanted to eat consciously—meaning with awareness of how food got to their plate.

✳ Skip ahead a few years. My husband and I were planning a dinner party for about twelve
friends who were not exactly the tofu and brown rice types (that, sadly, was about the
extent of my vegetarian culinary repertoire). My husband was not, and is not, vegan, but
by this time I had banished all animal products from the kitchen, and I was going a little
crazy trying to figure out what to serve the guests. I was poring over all my recipes and
fretting about whether a stir-fry would go over well (my husband assured me it would

not) when I remembered Tal. I was not a chef, to be sure, and I did not have a restaurant from which to carry out his compassionate cooking agenda, but our guests were leaders in the fields of media and business, so I thought I might have a shot at convincing him to come and cook for us. Thankfully, the soft-spoken and generous chef showed up at our door armed with groceries and a knockout menu.

The party was a smashing success. One of my favorite thank-you notes came from a very esteemed television journalist, who wrote, "The veal was the best I've ever had. Every single item was sublime. I look forward to more." Well, of course there had been no veal (and I was sure to tell him so); there had been nothing from any animals at all!

My husband was relieved (he had asked me not to mention to the guests that the meal was vegan so they wouldn't be wary), and so began my relationship with Tal and our shared mission of bringing consideration for animals into the kitchen. It's chefs like Tal who are leading the revolution in conscious cuisine; his exquisite, seasonal, and plant-based fare is simply some of the best food in the world.

It was not too long ago that eating a plant-based diet involved a bit of a sacrifice. Restaurant options were almost nonexistent, and a lot of vegetarian food tasted like cardboard. But for me the decision to cut out meat, then all animal products, had come out of a desire to live according to the values of kindness, compassion, and alleviating suffering when I could. A little sacrifice of flavor seemed more than worth it. But I still longed for sumptuous and satisfying meals.

As I looked into common practices of raising and killing animals for human consumption, I became sickened by the level of cruelty involved. The more I discovered by way of undercover videos and exposés on the subject, the more I became convinced that I simply could not eat anything that came from an animal. But I encountered so much resistance: Didn't I need meat and dairy to be healthy and strong? If eating animals is wrong, why do so many (good) people do it? And last but by no means least, what about taste and variety? Was I forever doomed to tasteless tofu and steamed vegetables with rice?

Fortunately, I quickly learned that not only could I do without animal protein but my health would in fact improve tremendously without all the problems associated with meat and dairy (high fat and cholesterol, carcinogenic proteins, salmonella, and additives like growth hormones and antibiotics).

Kathy Freston with Chef Tal

When I moved toward a plant-based diet, I lost weight and found myself with more energy—and my skin took on a glow I'd never seen as an omnivore. As for the question of why so many people eat animals and the argument that it's "natural" and has been done forever, I was reminded that humans were once sacrificed on altars, women were burned for being witches, and black people were sold into slavery. Thankfully, we evolve. We get smarter and more thoughtful, and ultimately we change.

"The food world has exploded over the past few years, and creative geniuses like Tal Ronnen are leading the way toward conscious and compassionate cooking."

In the case of our taste for vegetables and grains, we've come a very long way indeed. As many in the West have gotten more judicious about eating in a way that's consistent with our values, we have started looking not only at what not to eat but also at the great bounty we have to choose from. People are thinking more carefully than ever about where they spend their food dollars. The desire to buy locally produced foods is helping to fuel the national revival of farmers' markets. Adventurous eaters are trying less well-known grains like quinoa, vegetables like rutabagas, and new cooking methods to coax deep, delicious flavor out of the finest, freshest foods.

The food world has exploded over the past few years, and creative geniuses like Tal Ronnen are leading the way toward conscious and compassionate cooking.

Just thinking about Tal's Artichoke and Oyster Mushroom Rockefeller or his Tomato Bisque makes me swoon. His "Chicken" Scaloppini and Cornmeal-Crusted Tempeh bring me nearly to tears, they are so delicious. And I have won over many friends to this thoughtful way of eating with his marvelous Tempura Beet Rollatini.

Since Tal and I met, I've been blessed to have eaten dozens of meals prepared by him. I've often told friends that they simply have to try Tal's this or that. And now they can. Thank you, Tal, for bringing your exquisite vegan cuisine to the world—and helping us get smarter about food and practice compassion in the process. ✳

WELCOME,

✳ *I used to love steak.* Growing up, I ate it all the time, even as I sat across the table from two vegetarian sisters. When I crossed over to vegetarianism as a teenager, I didn't abandon my taste buds. I took them with me. In fact, I took them further. I became obsessed with the idea of creating vegan food that was just as mouth-watering and delicious as anything I'd ever had as a meat-eater. This book is my chance to share those discoveries with you. It's a guide to making satisfying, elegant meatless dishes that invite you to experience (and love) food in a whole new way.

I've been lucky enough to travel all around the world and work with amazing chefs in both classical and experimental restaurant kitchens. I've had the opportunity to soak up all sorts of cultures and flavors—and all of this has found its way into my cooking. The almond, persimmon, and fig trees outside my window in Israel, where I lived as a kid. The banana bread my American mother would bake. The Moroccan mincemeat "cigars" and hot peppers my babysitter cooked. The overstuffed pastrami sandwiches I had in Florida visiting my grandparents. The shabu shabu I'll never forget from my first trip to Japan. The falafel I ate every day for a month in New York City. The marinated and roasted eggplant of Carroll Gardens, Brooklyn. My love for Old Bay seasoning in Virginia. And hand-pulled ramen noodles in L.A.'s Little Tokyo. Every bite of it has influenced the recipes in this book.

Without pushing an agenda (okay, maybe I've pushed a bit), I've spread a little veganism wherever I've gone. I've become friends with chefs at the meatiest restaurants you can imagine, and shown them a few things that opened their minds (and their menus) to vegan options. It's easy to be convincing when the food is delicious. It doesn't feel like a sacrifice—it feels like a step up.

meat-eaters

There are no sprouts in this book, or in my refrigerator. I don't like them. I like rich, hearty meals, and I love cooking. I love being in the kitchen, alone or with friends. And this book is for people who feel the same—people who love to cook. Who want to get away from the microwave and spend some time enjoying the creativity of putting together beautiful, flavorful, unexpected dishes. Spending wonderful time together creating wonderful meals. I advocate a whole-foods diet consisting of unprocessed foods—it's the best thing for your body, and it's definitely the way I like to eat at home. But there are some good premade products that can help with the transition away from meat and dairy. I've included some of these in my recipes.

If you like hollandaise sauce, rich wine reductions, and meat-like textures, you'll like these recipes. There's a whole world out there of vegan cooking that's rich and delicious, like your favorite meat meals—but with no cholesterol and no animal anything. To prove it, and give you an even larger experience of the options, I've invited a few of my friends into this book—chefs who are doing really innovative, surprising things at incredible restaurants in London, L.A., and, believe it or not, Akron. See? It's happening everywhere. And it can happen in your own kitchen, too. Fun, beautiful, substantial vegan meals your friends and family will love. Whether you're interested in going all the way or are just vegan-curious, this is the perfect place to start.

I PROMISE, YOU WON'T MISS THE MEAT.

Chapter

1

You probably know the definition of "vegan," but here's how I like to put it: Being vegan means eating everything in the world except animal products. A positive spin, for sure, but this is a positive way to eat. This section answers a few common questions, dispels some myths, and, I hope, provides a bit of inspiration.

why VEGAN?

WITHOUT BEING PREACHY, here's a quick look at what veganism means to those who choose it. Even a step toward it—say, going meatless three days a week—lets you in on a lot of the benefits.

HEALTH Because cutting out animal products means virtually eliminating the risk of high cholesterol, high blood pressure, heart disease, and several types of cancer. Your energy shoots up and your weight is likely to drop.

ETHICS Because most of us question the morality of eating animals, and many people who feel it's absolutely wrong do it anyway out of habit. Eating with a clear conscience—feeling good about everything you put in your mouth—lightens up your life.

BECAUSE PAUL McCARTNEY SAYS SO: "If anyone wants to save the planet, all they have to do is just stop eating meat. That's the single most important thing you can do."

PLANET Because factory farming of animals consumes and pollutes insane quantities of water and demands so much feed that it threatens forests. And because greenhouse gases from animal emissions are destroying the atmosphere.

VEGANISM

BECAUSE ALBERT EINSTEIN SAID SO: "Nothing will benefit human health and increase chances for survival of life on Earth as much as the evolution to a vegetarian diet."

HELPING OTHERS Because the grain fed to livestock could feed at least twice as many hungry people in third-world countries. Weakening the livestock industry by buying less or no meat is a step toward rejiggering resources to save lives.

BUSTING THE TOP FIVE VEGAN *myths**

1. *myth:* "You won't get enough protein."

TRUTH: It's easy to get protein without eating any animal products. You just have to swap in plant proteins—tofu, tempeh, seitan, lentils, beans, whole grains—for the protein you used to get from meat. Most of us eat way more protein than we need anyway—somewhere around 100 grams a day. The FDA says we need 50 grams, and many nutrition experts say it's more like 30—that's covered in a serving of tofu with a side of quinoa. Done.

2. *myth:* "It's boring to eat vegan."

TRUTH: I get how it could seem that way. So help yourself out, as you might with any lifestyle shift: Find inspiration in recipe books, good vegetarian restaurants, and vegan friends. Take advantage of transitional meat-like foods, such as protein-rich Gardein, which I use in a few dishes (pages 118, 134, and 154). Change is hard, but if you go into this with a sense of the abundance of options rather than a feeling of lack, vegan cooking and eating will be anything but boring.

3. *myth:* "You'll be starving all the time."

TRUTH: There are plenty of hearty elements in a vegan diet, such as pasta and crusty bread, meaty mushrooms, and dense, filling soy-based proteins. Take a look at the entrée recipes, which start on page 132. They don't look like they'd leave you hungry, do they? A lot of people have an image in their heads of plates full of raw vegetables. Vegan eating is not that at all. It's just about dropping out the animal products. Everything else is there for you.

4. *myth:* "Giving up eggs and dairy is torture."

TRUTH: If you've decided not to eat chicken, I think it's only another half step to not eat eggs. From a health perspective, the cholesterol in just one egg pretty much maxes you out for the day. Cheese is a tough one. It's delicious, but it's probably the worst thing you can put in your body. Most of us can't comfortably digest dairy. Even if we don't get stomachaches from cheese, it can clog us up and make us feel phlegmy and slow. Plus, it's so high in cholesterol and saturated fat. Yes, for flavor, there's not much like cheese. But flavor-oriented vegan chefs like the friends I've profiled in this book have come up with ways to mimic the taste. With their help, I'll teach you how to use a few unexpected ingredients to get a cheesy taste in things like Caesar salad (page 56) and ravioli (page 146).

5. *myth:* "You have to go all the way or you shouldn't bother at all."

TRUTH: Even if you cut out animal products just two days a week, you can make a huge difference in your health and the health of the planet. Forcing a radical change that you won't be able to stick with doesn't make sense. Ease in at a pace and depth that feel comfortable. Beginning to eat vegan gives you a taste for it, and there's a good chance that if you do it part-time, you'll want to go further.

my favorite
PLANT-BASED
PROTEINS

quinoa is the "mother grain" of the Andes, and one of my favorites. Quick-cooking, with a nice crunch to it, quinoa is great in salads or as a substitute for white rice.

There's a common misconception that meatless meals are short on protein. This couldn't be further from the truth. Every entrée in this book has a delicious center-of-the-plate protein that packs a powerful nutritional punch—with no cholesterol. Switching over, even part-time, to vegan eating is about getting acquainted with all the wonderful plant-based proteins available.

nuts are most nutritious raw but much more flavorful roasted. You can buy raw nuts and easily slow-roast them yourself—that way you preserve the benefits and maximize the taste. Cook them in the toaster oven at 170°F for 15 minutes or so.

tofu may have gained a reputation as a cliché of vegetarian food, but it's incredibly versatile, and you won't believe how delicious it can be. I use silken tofu for creamy sauces, desserts, and dressings, and extra-firm for grilling and pan-frying, in all sorts of recipes.

edamame is just a name for soybeans that are picked early, while they're still soft. They're hard to find fresh, but you can buy them frozen, in the pod or out, just about anywhere. I prefer them in the pod, because they tend to retain more flavor. Add a little sea salt on the outside of the pods and kids will eat these up like pretzels.

lentils and other legumes, which include beans, split peas, and nuts, provide a tremendous amount of protein. They're also a major source of iron, calcium, zinc, and B vitamins. If you don't have time to cook up dried beans, canned organic beans are fine.

in my

KITCHEN:

Food processor
Indispensable for chopping and shredding vegetables, making dressings, and mixing dough.

French or Japanese knife, 10-inch
A great investment, because you'll use it constantly. Keep it very sharp. It's much safer that way. A dull knife tears and slips, and that's usually how people cut themselves. Some people think the honing rod (which often comes with knife sets) is for sharpening, but actually it's for re-aligning the edge of the knife when you have nicks. To sharpen the knife, you'll need a sharpening stone (which I recommend) or an electric sharpener. If you're cooking regu-larly, sharpen often. Wet the stone and sharpen on a 20-degree angle for a French knife, a 15-degree angle for a Japanese one.

Hands
I dress a salad with my hands, because they're gentle on the greens.

Japanese mandoline
I use this anytime I want something sliced very thin (like the beets for the rollatini on page 44) or really consistently. There's an attachment that does special cuts, like a julienne or a brunoise. This type of mando-line costs about a fifth of what a French one goes for.

Kitchen scissors
For cutting the ribs off chard and other greens. Much easier than using a knife.

KitchenAid mixer
Thanks to the attachments, this can do anything—pasta dough, mashed potatoes, icing. It's like having a second set of hands in the kitchen.

Plastic cutting board
Not wood. You don't want to cut on something hard, because it's tough on your knife. Plastic has a bit of give.

Pots and pans
Mine are stainless steel or copper. I don't like to use aluminum, though it's a better conductor of heat, because it's harder to clean. Copper's expensive, so a great compromise is stainless with a copper bottom.

Side towels
I use a lot of them, because I make a big mess when I cook.

Spatulas
Rubber for scraping, stainless for everything else.

Spice grinder
After a year, dry spices have lost most of their flavor. Instead, buy small amounts of fresh herbs (or better yet, grow them on the window-sill) and dry them yourself. I like to grind whole spices such as fennel seeds, peppercorns, coriander, cin-namon, mustard seeds, and even salt.

Squeeze bottles
For garnishing a dish with dressing or herb-infused oil, there's nothing that offers as much control.

Stainless steel tongs
I love plain old tongs. I always have a pair in one hand—to pick up a hot lid or grab a taste of something on the stove—and a side towel in the other.

Vita-Mix blender
I use this for everything—grinding grains, blending fruit, pureeing veg-etables. If you don't have one, use a Cuisinart or an immersion blender, but save your pennies in a jar in the kitchen, because the Vita-Mix is worth it. You'll love it. A regular blender might work, but in some recipes you will need a strainer to get a smooth texture. The Vita-Mix can grind things so fine that there's no grit. It just makes life so easy.

Wooden spoons
Great because they're nonreactive. It's good to have a couple that are extra long, for deep pots.

PANTRY:
SOME FAVORITE INGREDIENTS

Agar-agar
A great thickening agent made from red algae. Like gelatin, it has no taste.

Agave nectar
Derived from the agave cactus and similar to honey, this is a great sweetener for baking and sauces.

Almond milk
To pour on cereal and for dressings and sauces. I prefer it to soy milk.

Celtic sea salt
Kosher salt is really harsh in flavor. Sea salt is a lot gentler and sweeter. Unrefined salt, which is gray, is my favorite.

Coconut milk
Full-fat and organic—nice for sorbets, ice cream, and baking.

Curry pastes
I love them all—Thai red, green, and East Indian.

Dry and fresh herbs

Flaxseeds
Buy them whole, and shake them onto salad.

Grains
I especially love quinoa, millet, and brown rice.

Maple syrup

Miso paste

Nutritional yeast
Has a rich, nutty flavor and makes delicious cheesy sauces; can also be used in breading, dressings, and soups, as well as on pasta.

Oils
Olive oil: Great for marinades, dressings, and low-heat sautéeing. Canola oil: For frying, because of its high smoke point. Coconut oil: For richer, fattier flavor, instead of butter or lard. Sesame oil: To add flavor at the end of cooking, especially to Asian dishes.

Panko bread crumbs

Vegetarian stock
A basic vegetable stock, plus a roasted stock for darker sauces. Best is homemade, if you have time—just cook up all the vegetable scraps from the week.

Vinegars
Champagne vinegar: Lighter than other vinegars and especially nice on citrus. Regular and white balsamic vinegar: White balsamic is milder. Rice vinegar: Great for Asian-style dishes.

Whole wheat pasta

A few of my favorite brands

Earth Balance
The absolute best butter substitute there is. It's made from really good oils—olive, soy, canola—is non-hydrogenated, and it's cold-pressed, not processed with heat. I like original, not whipped, or the Vegan Buttery Sticks.

Muir Glen
Fire Roasted Tomatoes
The brand I use when I make my Tomato Bisque (page 94).

Wildwood Soy Yogurt
The only plain soy yogurt I know of that doesn't have sweetener in it. It's actually tart. You can use it for savory applications, like in dressings or blended with a tandoori spice mix, or a dollop tossed in soups.

Red Palm Oil
by Jungle Products
For giving a yolky color to things like homemade pasta. It has a smoky flavor, so use just a little.

Vegenaise
My favorite vegan mayo. It's in the refrigerated section at the store, and you'll see it in a couple of the sandwich recipes in this book.

my favorite
SUPER**FOODS**

We've all heard about foods that pack an amazing nutritional punch—the ones that stand out for their health properties. I personally feel that all whole foods do that, and that if you eat a variety of them, your body will get everything it needs. Here are some of my favorites from the superfoods category.

pomegranates The easiest way to get seeds out is to cut the fruit in half and spank the back with a wooden spoon. They pop right out.

spinach High in calcium, and great when juiced with carrots and parsley.

blueberries Fresh-picked with a squirt of lemon, there's no better summer treat.

flaxseeds Known for fighting all sorts of diseases, they're easy to work into your diet. Sprinkle them on salads for crunch. I prefer them whole rather than ground.

chocolate Most people think chocolate isn't vegan, but high-quality dark chocolate usually is. Check the label for dairy—milk is always listed if it's in there, because it's a common allergen.

broccoli Full of calcium. I love it in a creamy soup.

avocados I prefer Haas (the smaller, dark green variety) to Florida avocados (the brighter ones), because they have much more flavor.

MEET

CASHEW *cream*

THE MAGIC INGREDIENT THAT MAKES IT
EASY TO LIVE WITHOUT DAIRY

If you've thumbed through the recipes in this book, you've seen the ingredient "cashew cream" a few times. It's a vegan-chef staple that stands in for dairy in a variety of ways. In the raw-food world, where it originated, it's used in lots of desserts. When you cook with it, though, it can be so much more—from cheese filling in ravioli to heavy cream in soups. It can be stored 2 to 3 days in the refrigerator and can be frozen for up to 6 months (although after it's defrosted it can be a bit lumpy, so it's good to give it a spin in the blender to smooth it out before using it).

The trick when making cashew cream is to use raw cashews. They have no flavor of their own; they're just a vessel for fat and creaminess. (It's the roasting that brings out the familiar sweetness in cashews.) Because it has a nice fat content, cashew cream reduces in a pan even faster than heavy cream. (Soy milk, which some people use in vegan cooking, has no fat, so it doesn't reduce into a thick sauce—it's really not an alternative.)

For different applications, there are different consistencies—thick and regular. (I've also included a recipe for Whipped Cashew Cream, which is a great accompaniment to desserts.) Both are easy to make but not quick, because the cashews need to soak overnight. A shortcut is to put the cashews in a pot with water, bring them to a boil, then shut off the heat and let them soak for an hour. But this starts to leach out the sweetness, so you're better off with the overnight method. Also, there's at least one decent brand of store-bought nut cream, called Mimic Cream, which combines cashews and almonds; you can usually find it on the shelves or in the refrigerated section near the soy milk. Of course, nothing compares to homemade, and once you get used to it, there may be no turning back.

regular and thick cashew cream

2 cups whole raw cashews (not pieces, which are often dry),
  rinsed very well under cold water

Put the cashews in a bowl and add cold water to cover them. Cover the
bowl and refrigerate overnight.

Drain the cashews and rinse under cold water. Place in a blender
with enough fresh cold water to cover them by 1 inch. Blend on high for
several minutes until very smooth. (If you're not using a professional
high-speed blender such as a Vita-Mix, which creates an ultra-smooth
cream, strain the cashew cream through a fine-mesh sieve.)

To make thick cashew cream, which some of the recipes in this book
call for, simply reduce the amount of water in the blender, so that the
water just covers the cashews.

Makes about 2¼ cups thick cream or 3½ cups regular cream
Prep time: 10 minutes, plus soaking overnight

whipped cashew cream

1 cup thick cashew cream (see above)
¼ cup light agave nectar
½ teaspoon vanilla extract
⅔ cup refined coconut oil, warmed until liquid

Place the cashew cream in a blender and add the agave nectar, vanilla,
and ¼ cup water. Blend until thoroughly combined.

With the blender running, slowly drizzle the coconut oil in through
the hole in the blender lid. Blend until emulsified.

Pour into a bowl and chill in the refrigerator, covered, for 2 hours.
Stir before serving.

Makes about 2 cups
Prep time: 5 minutes, plus 2 hours chilling

Chapter

Most of the recipes in this section work as finger food, so they're great for everything from a cocktail party to a Super Bowl get-together. I've used many of them for sophisticated celebrity weddings, but they're not too fancy to bring to a potluck or to serve as a first course at a casual dinner for friends.

STARTERS & SMALL PLATES:

Twice-Baked Fingerling Potatoes with Crisped Dulse (p30) *Grilled Artichokes with Caesar Dressing* (p32) Shiso Bites (p34) *Artichoke and Oyster Mushroom Rockefeller* (p38) Ponzu-Glazed Tofu Crystal Rolls (p40) *Quinoa Maki with Avocado and Cajun Portobello Fillets* (p42) Tempura Beet Rollatini with Balsamic Gastrique (p44) *Sweet Onion Beggar's Purses* (p46) Fresh-Baked Focaccia with Caramelized Onions (p50) ✳

twice-baked
fingerling potatoes *with*
crisped dulse

This is an upgrade of a very easy, old-fashioned recipe—the twice-baked potato. In this version, you get the richness from cashew cream spiked with horseradish and the sea vegetable dulse. If you're not a fan of horseradish, skip it and fold in fresh herbs instead.

❋

Good at room temperature, so you can make them a bit ahead of time.

"These are tiny treats—two bites each, savory and delicious. But you can use the same recipe for Yukon golds or new potatoes."

12 fingerling potatoes,
   cleaned and dried
2 teaspoons prepared horseradish
1 tablespoon vegan mayonnaise
2 tablespoons regular
   Cashew Cream (page 26)

Sea salt and freshly ground
   black pepper
1 tablespoon Earth Balance
Paprika
2 tablespoons minced
   fresh chives
Crisped Dulse (recipe follows)

1   Preheat the oven to 350°F. Place the potatoes on a baking sheet coated with spray oil and bake for 20 minutes, or until tender. Meanwhile, in a small bowl, stir together the horseradish, mayonnaise, Cashew Cream, and salt and pepper to taste.

2   Cut the cooked potatoes in half lengthwise. Being careful not to burn your fingers, scoop the pulp from each potato with a teaspoon, leaving a thin shell. Place the potato pulp in the bowl with the horseradish mixture and the Earth Balance. Mash together, then fill each potato half with the mixture, mounding slightly. Put the potato halves filling side up on the baking sheet.

3   Sprinkle the potatoes with paprika, return to the oven, and bake for 10 more minutes. Garnish with the chives and Crisped Dulse.

Makes 24 pieces; 12 servings
Prep time: 45 minutes

* crisped **dulse**

1 teaspoon canola oil
1 or 2 small pieces dulse

Heat the oil in a small nonstick pan over medium heat. Add the dulse and cook, turning once or twice, until crisp, 1 to 2 minutes. Watch closely so that it doesn't burn.
   Remove the dulse to paper towels, let cool, then break into small pieces.

grilled artichokes
with caesar dressing

I first served this dish at the restaurant Sublime, in Fort Lauderdale. These are great cooked outside on the grill, but it's fine just to use a grill pan in the kitchen, too. Make a lot—everyone will devour them.

2 fresh whole artichokes, trimmed
4 teaspoons olive oil
½ cup roughly chopped fresh parsley
1 large garlic clove

Zest of ½ lemon
¼ teaspoon red pepper flakes
Salt and pepper
Caesar Dressing (recipe follows)

1. Pour 1 inch of water into a steamer pot and bring to a boil. Place the artichokes in the steamer with the tips facing up, cover, and cook for 30 to 40 minutes, or until an inside leaf can be pulled out easily. Let cool.

2. Cut the artichokes in half from top to bottom (a very sharp serrated knife works best for this) and drizzle the insides with the oil.

3. Finely mince the parsley, garlic, and lemon zest together, add the red pepper flakes and salt and pepper to taste, then sprinkle the mixture over the cut halves of the artichokes.

4. Preheat a charcoal grill to high, or heat a grill pan over medium-high heat. Grill the artichokes cut side down until lightly blackened, 3 to 5 minutes. Serve with Caesar Dressing for dipping.

Makes 4 servings
Prep time: 1 hour

✳ caesar dressing

1 garlic clove
1 teaspoon capers, drained
⅓ cup vegan mayonnaise
1 teaspoon white miso paste

1½ teaspoons nutritional yeast flakes
½ teaspoon light agave nectar
1 tablespoon fresh lemon juice
½ cup olive oil

Put the garlic, capers, mayonnaise, miso paste, nutritional yeast, agave nectar, lemon juice, and 2 tablespoons water in a food processor and pulse to combine.

With the motor running, slowly add the oil in a thin stream. Continue to blend for 1 minute.

shiso bites

These are so easy—a 10-minute recipe but really refreshing and striking on the plate. Shiso is a Japanese leaf with a peppery, minty flavor. The ingredients inside—cayenne and citrus—have a sort of zing to them, and you just fold the leaf in half like a little roll-up and pop it in your mouth.

6 fresh shiso leaves
¼ cup peeled and julienned fresh daikon
½ cup finely shredded napa cabbage
6 grapefruit segments
1 tablespoon extra-virgin olive oil
Sea salt
Ground cayenne
Black and white sesame seeds

1   Place each shiso leaf on a separate salad plate and divide the daikon and cabbage among them, then top each with a grapefruit segment.

2   Drizzle with the oil and season with salt and cayenne. Sprinkle with the sesame seeds. Serve them flat, but eat them rolled up like a taco.

Makes 6 servings
Prep time: 10 minutes

＊

Black and white sesame seeds add texture and crunch.

my favorite
CITRUS

I use citrus all the time, for dressings and marinades and as a refreshing component in winter salads. No matter which fruit you're working with, the zest is full of fragrant essential oils—great for punching up flavors in all sorts of dishes. You always want to use organic fruit when possible, but especially for zest, because you don't want skin that's been treated with pesticides. The trick to zesting is to not push so deep into the fruit that you get the pith—the bitter white part between skin and flesh. Stay on the surface for the best result.

ugli fruit

pomelo

tangerine

grapefruit

mandarin orange

kaffir lime leaves

blood orange

lime

lemon

meyer lemon

kumquats

artichoke *and* oyster mushroom rockefeller

I like the challenge of making something you'd never imagine you could have in a vegan diet. It's fun to do that with the vessel, too, to extend the experience beyond just the food. Here you get something that looks like a seafood appetizer, plus all the rich flavors associated with it. Nori gives the oyster mushrooms a slight seafood taste.

*

The artichoke leaf stands in for the oyster shell, but the bonus is that you get a nice bit of artichoke, too.

1 whole globe artichoke

Sea salt

6 tablespoons Earth Balance

½ cup very finely minced spinach leaves,
from 4 ounces spinach (4 cups packed)

3 tablespoons finely minced onion

3 tablespoons finely minced fresh parsley

5 tablespoons bread crumbs

Dash of Tabasco sauce

½ teaspoon anise-flavored liqueur
(such as Herbsaint or Pernod)

1 tablespoon olive oil

8 ounces oyster mushrooms,
stems removed

¼ sheet nori seaweed, toasted and ground
to a fine powder (see page 140, step 3)

Rock salt

Strips of lemon zest, lemon wedges

1   Pour 1 inch of water into a steamer pot and bring to a boil. Place the artichoke in the steamer basket with the tip facing up, cover, and cook for 30 to 40 minutes, or until an inside leaf can be pulled out easily. Let cool.

2   Place a medium sauté pan over medium heat. Sprinkle the bottom with a pinch of sea salt and heat for 1 minute. Add the Earth Balance and let it melt and coat the pan, being careful not to let it burn. This will create a nonstick effect. Add the spinach, onion, parsley, bread crumbs, Tabasco sauce, liqueur, and a pinch of sea salt. Cook for 10 minutes, stirring occasionally, or until the onion is soft but the mixture is not browned. Press the spinach mixture in a fine-mesh sieve to remove the excess liquid.

3   Place a medium sauté pan over medium heat. Sprinkle the bottom with a pinch of sea salt and heat for 1 minute. Add the oil and heat for 30 seconds, being careful not to let it smoke. Add the mushrooms and sauté, seasoning with the nori powder, until they have released their liquid and are nicely browned and crisp on the outside, 5 to 7 minutes.

4   Preheat the broiler to high. Pour a layer of rock salt, about ¼ inch deep, on a large ovenproof plate or serving platter. Remove the artichoke leaves from the steamed artichoke and lay 1 for each mushroom you have on the plate, nestling them in the rock salt. Place 1 mushroom in each leaf and cover with the spinach mixture.

5   Broil about 4 inches from the heat source for about 3 minutes, until heated through, being careful not to burn the artichoke leaves. Garnish with the lemon zest and serve with the lemon wedges.

Makes 6 servings
Prep time: 1 hour

ponzu-glazed
tofu crystal rolls

These are like a Japanese version of Thai spring rolls. They're classic, in a sense—the fresh Vietnamese style of rice paper with cabbage, carrots, and tofu. But the tofu is baked in a ponzu marinade (a citrus-flavored soy sauce), and that's what makes it taste Japanese.

¼ cup ponzu

1 pound firm tofu, cut into 8 (¼-inch-thick) slabs

1 tablespoon sesame oil

3 garlic cloves, minced

1 thumb-sized piece ginger, peeled and minced

2 tablespoons soy sauce

¼ head cabbage, shredded

2 scallions, chopped

2 carrots, peeled and grated

5 (8-inch) round rice paper sheets (spring roll skins), soaked in warm water for 5 minutes

2 ounces rice vermicelli, soaked separately in warm water for 10 minutes, then drained

25 fresh mint leaves

Miso Sambal Sauce (recipe follows)

1   Preheat the oven to 375°F. Pour the ponzu into a 9 by 13-inch baking dish. Place the tofu slabs in a single layer in the baking dish. Turn over to coat with the ponzu. Bake for 20 minutes, turning the tofu over halfway through. Let cool, then cut into ¼-inch-wide strips.

2   Heat the oil in a large sauté pan over medium heat. Add the garlic and ginger and sauté for 30 seconds. Add the soy sauce, cabbage, scallions, and carrots and sauté for 5 minutes, or until the vegetables are soft and wilted. Let cool.

3   To assemble the rolls, remove a sheet of rice paper from the water, shake to remove the excess water, and place on a flat surface. Put one or two strips of tofu, some of the cabbage mixture, some of the vermicelli, and 5 mint leaves across one end of the rice paper sheet. Roll up tightly. The roll should be about 1 inch in diameter.

4   Cut each roll into 4 or 5 pieces, place each piece faceup on a plate, and garnish each piece with a small dollop of the Miso Sambal Sauce.

Makes 20 to 25 pieces; 6 servings
Prep time: 45 minutes

✳ miso sambal **sauce**

2 tablespoons yellow miso paste

1 tablespoon sambal oelek (Thai chile sauce)

1 teaspoon light agave nectar

Mix all the ingredients together in a small bowl.

quinoa maki *with* avocado *and* cajun portobello fillets

This is a different take on sushi. The blackened mushroom is crispy and spicy, and the avocado offers a nice cooling contrast. Instead of white rice, which isn't very nutritious, I use quinoa. It has a lot of protein and a great toothsome texture.

2 tablespoons vegan mayonnaise
1 tablespoon sambal oelek
    (Thai chile sauce)
1 cup quinoa, cooked in water
    according to package directions
    and cooled to room temperature
2 teaspoons rice vinegar

1 teaspoon sugar
5 or 6 nori sheets
1 avocado, cut into ¼-inch-thick slices
2 Cajun portobello fillets (page 112),
    cut into ¼-inch-thick slices
2 scallions, chopped
Soy sauce

1   In a small bowl, mix together the vegan mayonnaise and sambal oelek. Set aside.

2   In a medium bowl, stir together the quinoa, vinegar, and sugar. Spread a thin layer of the mixture on a sheet of nori, covering the sheet except for a 1-inch space along the far edge of the sheet. On the full length of the near end of the nori sheet, place single strips of avocado and portobello, a sprinkle of scallions, and small dollops of the sambal mixture.

3   Moisten the clean edge of the nori sheet with a bit of water. Beginning at the filled end, roll up the nori sheet very tightly (you may want to use a sushi mat). Press firmly when you get to the moistened edge to seal the roll. Repeat with the remaining nori and filling. Cut each roll into 6 pieces. Serve with soy sauce for dipping.

Makes 4 entrée servings or 8 appetizer servings
Prep time: 15 minutes, not including quinoa cooking and cooling

tempura beet rollatini *with* balsamic gastrique

This is a fun recipe. White balsamic has a milder taste than the more common dark kind, and I like to use it when boiling beets because it doesn't compete with the flavor of the vegetable. Once the beets are cooked, you slice them thin, fill them with tofu ricotta, dip them in tempura batter, and fry them. The red bleeds through the batter for a pretty presentation. And they're just delicious.

1 large red beet, scrubbed
¼ cup white balsamic vinegar
8 ounces firm tofu, pressed well in a towel
   to remove most of the moisture
1½ teaspoons nutritional yeast flakes
½ teaspoon dried granulated onion
Juice of ½ lemon
½ cup thick Cashew Cream (page 26)

1½ teaspoons white miso paste
Sea salt and freshly ground
   black pepper
1 cup vegan tempura batter mix
1 tablespoon minced fresh chives
Canola oil
Balsamic Gastrique (recipe follows)

1. Place the beet in a small pot and cover with water. Add the white balsamic vinegar. Bring to a boil and cook until fork-tender, about 40 minutes. Meanwhile, place the tofu, nutritional yeast, onion, lemon juice, Cashew Cream, miso paste, ½ teaspoon salt, and ⅛ teaspoon pepper in a food processor and blend until the mixture has the texture of ricotta cheese.

2. In a small bowl, prepare the tempura batter according to the package directions, then fold in the chives, 1 teaspoon salt, and ¼ teaspoon pepper.

3. Hold the cooked beet under cold running water until cool. Peel off the skin (a soup spoon works well). Slice the beet paper-thin on a mandoline. Dry the slices with paper towels and season on both sides with salt and pepper. Spread a small, mounded strip of the tofu ricotta mixture on one end of each beet slice and roll up; use a dab of the ricotta mixture to hold the roll closed if necessary.

4. Pour 2 inches of oil into a large, heavy pot and heat to 375°F. Holding a roll together, dip in the tempura batter, coating thoroughly, and carefully lower into the oil. Fry the rolls, a few at a time to avoid crowding the pot, until well browned and crisp, about 2 minutes. Remove to a pan lined with paper towels and set aside in a warm oven until all the rolls are fried. Serve hot, drizzled with the Balsamic Gastrique.

Makes about 24 rollatini; 6 servings
Prep time: 1 hour, 15 minutes

✳ balsamic gastrique

2 cups balsamic vinegar
¼ cup sugar

In a small saucepan over medium-high heat, stir together the vinegar and sugar. Cook until syrupy and reduced by two thirds, about 15 minutes.

sweet onion
beggar's purses

This is an elegant recipe for a relaxed afternoon in the kitchen. It's like making onion marmalade. You cook down the onions for a long time, then add balsamic vinegar, brown sugar, and mustard. It's yummy and great to serve to friends because it makes such a beautiful plate.

For the onion jam:

Sea salt
¼ cup canola oil
2½ pounds red onions, thinly sliced
¼ cup lightly packed dark
   brown sugar
¾ cup balsamic vinegar
¾ cup red wine
3 tablespoons whole-grain
   Dijon mustard

For the purses:

16 sheets (about ½ box) dairy-free
   frozen phyllo dough, thawed for
   2 hours at room temperature
½ cup Earth Balance, melted
Freshly ground black pepper
⅓ cup chopped fresh thyme
24 chives

1   *Make the onion jam:* Place a large flat-bottomed pan over medium heat. Sprinkle the bottom with a pinch of salt and heat for 1 minute. Add the oil and heat for 1 minute, being careful not to let it smoke. This will create a nonstick effect. Add the onions and cook over medium-low heat for 20 to 25 minutes, or until golden brown, stirring occasionally. Add the brown sugar and cook for 5 minutes.

2   Stir in the vinegar, wine, and 2 teaspoons salt and continue to cook for 20 to 25 minutes, or until the onions are reduced by about three quarters and are the consistency of jam. Remove from the heat and stir in the mustard, thyme, and pepper to taste.

3   *Make the purses:* Preheat the oven to 375°F. Unroll the phyllo dough and lay 1 sheet flat on a work surface; rewrap the dough you're not working with to keep it from drying out. Using a pastry brush, brush the entire surface of the sheet with melted Earth Balance.

4   Lay another sheet on top, brush with Earth Balance, and repeat until you have 4 layers of phyllo dough. Season with black pepper and chopped thyme between every other layer. Using a pastry cutter or pizza wheel, cut the phyllo into 6 (4½-inch) squares. Repeat with the remaining phyllo sheets to make 24 squares. Place about 1 tablespoon of the onion jam in the center of each square. Draw up the edges of the phyllo to create a rough purse. Gently twist the packet just above the pocket containing the jam to create frills at the top.

5   Tie each purse with kitchen string and brush the entire purse lightly with melted Earth Balance. Place them on a parchment-lined baking sheet and bake for 15 to 20 minutes, or until well browned. Meanwhile, blanch the chives for 1 minute in boiling water, then cool. When the purses are cooked, carefully remove the string from the purses and tie a chive around each.

Makes 24 purses; 6 servings
Prep time: 1 hour, 45 minutes

my favorite
HERBS

thyme

Even though they're subtle, herbs can have a huge effect on a dish. The sense memories attached to certain herbs call to mind meat dishes—sage reminds people of sausage, and rosemary is reminiscent of roast chicken. That's one of the tricks for bringing "meaty" flavor to vegetable-based cooking. Whenever possible, use fresh herbs. Generally, you want to add fresh ones late in a recipe and dry ones early in the cooking process. Also, adjust your measurements: A tablespoon of fresh herbs equals about a teaspoon of dry.

basil

rosemary

saffron

chives

sage

mint

fresh-baked focaccia *with* caramelized onions

These days you can get good fresh baguettes or whole-grain loaves at so many bakeries, but it's a real treat to fill your house with the cozy aroma of baking bread. You can do a lot with this recipe. Try adding some grilled fennel and cracked pepper at the last minute. Or sprinkle the focaccia with zatar, a Middle Eastern spice blend, and top with a few slices of oil-packed Greek olives.

1 tablespoon sugar
1½ cups warm water
1 packet active dry yeast
6 cups unbleached all-purpose flour
Sea salt
⅓ cup plus ¼ cup extra-virgin olive oil

1 tablespoon Earth Balance
2 red onions, thinly sliced
½ teaspoon red pepper flakes
1 teaspoon dried rosemary needles
½ teaspoon freshly ground
   black pepper

1 Place the sugar in a large bowl or the bowl of a stand mixer fitted with a dough hook. Pour the warm water over the sugar and stir to dissolve. Sprinkle the yeast over the water and let it sit without stirring for 15 minutes so the yeast can activate (it should appear bubbly on the surface). If it does not bubble, the yeast is not viable; start again with new yeast.

2 In a separate bowl, mix the flour and 1 tablespoon salt. Add the flour mixture, about 1 cup at a time, and the ⅓ cup oil, a spoonful or two at a time, to the yeast mixture. Stir with a wooden spoon or mix on low speed to combine.

3 Turn the dough out onto a floured work surface and knead for 10 minutes (or continue to knead on low speed in the mixer for 10 minutes), or until a firm, smooth dough forms. Place the dough in an oiled bowl, turning over to coat with oil. Cover with a damp cloth and let rise in a warm place for 1½ hours.

4 Meanwhile, place a sauté pan over medium heat. Sprinkle the bottom with a pinch of salt and heat for 1 minute. Add 1 tablespoon of the remaining oil and the Earth Balance and heat for 30 seconds, being careful not to let it smoke. This will create a nonstick effect. Add the onions to the pan and sauté, stirring frequently, until very soft and browned, 20 to 25 minutes. Set aside.

5 Line a baking sheet with parchment paper. Brush or spray the parchment with oil. Turn the dough out onto the parchment and pull and stretch it with your hands to fill the pan. The dough should stretch to the edges of the pan and be about ¼ inch thick. Use your fingertips to make dimples all over the dough, about 1 inch apart. Do not otherwise press the dough. Let rise, covered, for another 20 minutes.

6 Preheat the oven to 400°F. In a small bowl, stir together the remaining 3 tablespoons oil, the red pepper flakes, rosemary, 2 teaspoons salt, and the black pepper. Brush the top of the dough with the oil mixture. Bake for 7 minutes, then rotate the pan front to back, spread the onions over the top, and bake for another 8 to 10 minutes, or until golden and crusty. Remove the dough to a cutting board, let cool for at least 10 minutes, then cut into squares.

Makes 1 large loaf; 6 to 8 servings
Prep time: 2 hours (some unattended), plus 1½ hours rising

Chapter

For me the best thing about salads is making dressings from scratch. These recipes contain a lot of really great dressings, plus some interesting vegetables that might be new to you. Salads are especially nutritious, of course, because most or all of the ingredients are raw. But it doesn't hurt to throw in some nice roasted beets or savory little roasted potatoes.

SALADS: Green Bean and Fingerling Potato Salad with Miso Dressing(p55) *Caesar Salad with Focaccia Croutons*(p56) Fresh Mint and Cucumber Salad with Tahini Vinaigrette(p58) *Heirloom Tomato Salad with Crisped Capers*(p61) Quinoa, Avocado, and Sweet Potato Timbale with Roasted Tomatillo Dressing(p64) *Bibb Lettuce, Shaved Fennel, and Grapefruit Salad with Pickled Onion*(p70) Summer Chopped Salad(p72) *Orange, Belgian Endive, and Quinoa Salad with Champagne Vinaigrette*(p74) Very Green Salad with Cucumber, Kohlrabi, Sweet Onion and Herb Vinaigrette(p77) ✳

The miso flavor is unexpected but delicious.

green bean *and* fingerling potato salad *with* miso dressing

Potatoes always need to be well coated or they'll be dry—and this thick, savory dressing does a good job of that. And what's better than green beans and potatoes together? It's a classic combination, with a twist in the dressing.

2 tablespoons yellow miso paste
3 tablespoons rice vinegar
1 tablespoon light agave nectar
¼ teaspoon sea salt
¼ teaspoon freshly ground black pepper
½ shallot, minced
1 garlic clove, minced
1 tablespoon Dijon mustard
Juice of ½ lemon

½ cup safflower oil
1 tablespoon minced fresh chives
1½ cups baby arugula
8 ounces fingerling potatoes, boiled for 15 minutes, then sliced into ¼-inch-thick rounds
8 ounces green beans, blanched in boiling water for 1 minute

1   Place the miso paste, vinegar, agave nectar, salt, pepper, shallot, garlic, mustard, lemon juice, and 1 tablespoon water in a food processor and pulse to combine. With the motor running, slowly add the oil in a thin stream until the vinaigrette is emulsified. Fold in the chives.

2   Place the arugula, potatoes, and beans in a large bowl, drizzle with the vinaigrette, and toss to coat.

Makes 4 servings
Prep time: 30 minutes

caesar salad
with focaccia croutons

This is an easy recipe and utilizes some of my favorite tricks. To get the briny flavor of anchovies, I use capers. Nutritional yeast replaces Parmesan—on its own it doesn't taste like cheese, but miso gives it the traditional flavor. Vegenaise, an amazing mayo substitute, is the base of the dressing. These key ingredients give this salad the intensity of a true Caesar.

¼ plain focaccia, cut into ½-inch cubes
3 cloves garlic
1 tablespoon capers, drained
1 cup vegan mayonnaise
1 tablespoon white miso paste
2 tablespoons nutritional yeast flakes
½ tablespoon light agave nectar

1 cup olive oil
Sea salt and freshly ground
    black pepper
2 small heads romaine
    lettuce, shredded
Caperberries

1   Preheat the oven to 350°F. Spread the focaccia cubes on a baking sheet and bake for 10 minutes, or until lightly toasted.

2   In a food processor, mince the garlic and capers. Add the mayonnaise, miso paste, nutritional yeast, agave nectar, and ½ cup water and pulse to combine. With the motor running, slowly add the oil in a thin stream. Continue to blend until emulsified, about 1 minute. Season with salt and pepper to taste.

3   Place the lettuce and croutons in a large bowl. Drizzle the dressing over the top and toss well to coat. Garnish with caperberries and serve immediately.

Makes 4 servings
Prep time: 15 minutes

fresh mint *and* cucumber salad *with* tahini vinaigrette

This is a simple salad since it's really only cucumbers and mint—a very focused dish. With soy yogurt in the dressing, plus fresh mint, it definitely has a Middle Eastern feel. And it's as easy as it looks. It would make a great lunch with the Mediterranean Chickpea Wrap (page 122).

For the tahini vinaigrette:

2 tablespoons tahini
¾ cup grapeseed oil
¼ cup freshly squeezed lemon juice
2 teaspoons minced shallot
1 small garlic clove, minced

2 tablespoons light agave nectar
¾ cup plain soy yogurt
¼ cup white wine vinegar
Pinch of ground cayenne
Sea salt

For the salad:

1 English cucumber, peeled and
    thinly sliced
1 tablespoon minced fresh mint
1 tablespoon minced fresh parsley

1   *Make the tahini vinaigrette:* Combine the tahini, oil, lemon juice, shallot, garlic, agave nectar, soy yogurt, vinegar, and ¼ cup water in a blender and puree until smooth, adding more water if necessary to make the dressing pourable. Add the cayenne and season with salt to taste.

2   *Make the salad:* Place the cucumber in a small bowl, top with enough of the dressing to coat generously, sprinkle with the mint and parsley, and toss to combine.

Makes 2 servings
Prep time: 15 minutes

*

Save the remaining dressing for drizzling over vegetables in a pita.

The capers add a nice savory element, plus some crunch.

heirloom tomato salad
with crisped capers

This summery dish is all about highlighting fresh tomatoes. "Heirloom" refers to certain cultivars that have been nurtured and preserved for generations, and any varieties that you like will do. The capers add a nice savory element, plus some crunch.

¼ cup plus 1 teaspoon extra-virgin olive oil
1 tablespoon capers, drained
3 pounds mixed heirloom tomatoes, cut into ½-inch wedges
2 tablespoons fresh basil chiffonade
Sea salt and freshly ground black pepper

1   Heat 1 teaspoon of the oil in a small sauté pan over medium-high heat. Add the capers and cook until crisp, 1 to 2 minutes. Remove to a paper towel.

2   Place the tomatoes in a large bowl. Drizzle with the remaining ¼ cup oil, add the basil, season with salt and pepper to taste, and gently toss to coat. Sprinkle the capers on the salads after they're plated so they stay crisp.

Makes 6 servings
Prep time: 10 minutes

my favorite
GREENS

tuscan kale I'd rather have this than almost any other cooked green. It's my favorite, for both flavor and texture. Once in a while I'll deep-fry it for about three seconds as a snack. It's also great to munch raw.

Cultures that don't rely on dairy for calcium often get it through leafy greens like these. Raw greens are also packed with iron— the deeper the hue, the more nutritious.

arugula Baby arugula is easy for salads because it doesn't have hard stems. I use various kinds, though, in cooked recipes. I love them all.

dandelion greens It's nice to toss these in with a milder lettuce for a bitter, peppery bite in a salad. I also like them quickly sautéed.

quinoa, avocado, *and* sweet potato timbale *with* roasted tomatillo dressing

I made this dish for the reopening of a Fort Lauderdale restaurant called Sublime, and it became one of the best-selling salads there. Sublime is a great place owned by animal activist Nanci Alexander—she gives all the profits to organizations that promote animal welfare and a vegan lifestyle. This salad is hearty, thanks to the sweet potato and quinoa, and also makes an impressive presentation.

For the quinoa:

1 cup quinoa, cooked in vegetable
    stock according to package directions
    and cooled to room temperature
½ jalapeño, minced
1 tablespoon minced fresh cilantro
1 tablespoon extra-virgin olive oil
Juice of 1 lime
Salt and freshly ground black pepper
    to taste

For the sweet potatoes:

1 sweet potato, peeled and cut
    into ½-inch dice
2 teaspoons extra-virgin olive oil
Sea salt and freshly ground black pepper

For the dresssing:

2 tomatillos in olive oil, skins removed
3 tablespoons plus 1 teaspoon olive oil
1 tablespoon rice vinegar
¼ cup chopped fresh cilantro
1 teaspoon light agave nectar
Sea salt and freshly ground black pepper

For the tortilla strips:

Canola oil
2 corn tortillas, cut into ¼-inch strips
1 teaspoon Cajun seasoning

To serve:

2 avocados, diced
Microgreens

1 *Make the quinoa:* Place all of the quinoa ingredients in a medium bowl and toss to combine.

2 *Make the sweet potatoes:* Preheat the oven to 400°F. In a small bowl, toss the sweet potatoes with the oil, and season with salt and pepper to taste. Spread in a single layer on a baking sheet and roast for 15 minutes, or until soft in the middle and lightly browned; be careful not to let the sweet potatoes burn.

3 *Make the dressing:* Lower the oven temperature to 350°F. In a small bowl, toss the tomatillos with 1 teaspoon of the oil. Place on a baking sheet and roast for 15 minutes. Transfer to a food processor, add the vinegar, cilantro, and agave nectar, and pulse to combine. With the motor running, pour in the remaining 3 tablespoons oil in a thin stream. Continue blending until emulsified. Season with salt and pepper to taste.

"This salad is hearty, thanks to the sweet potato and quinoa, and also makes an impressive presentation."

4 *Make the tortilla strips:* Pour 2 inches of oil into a small, heavy pot and heat until the oil shimmers. Add the tortilla strips and fry until crisp and browned, 1 to 2 minutes. Drain on paper towels and sprinkle with the Cajun seasoning.

5 *Assemble the salads:* Place a 3-inch ring mold in the center of one of 4 salad plates. Fill with ¼ of the quinoa mixture and press down with a spoon to pack the mold, smoothing the top. Place ¼ of the sweet potato pieces on top of the quinoa and press down gently. Top with ¼ of the avocado and press down gently. Carefully remove the mold. Repeat on the remaining salad plates.

6 Carefully place 2 tortilla strips parallel to each other about 1 inch apart on top of each timbale. Place 2 more tortilla strips perpendicular on top of those. Top the timbales with the microgreens and drizzle the dressing around the timbales.

Makes 4 servings
Prep time: 45 minutes

THE QUINOA SMUGGLER: Don McKinley

BOULDER, CO

I don't know what I'd do without quinoa, the incredibly nutritious "Mother Grain of the Andes." It's a delicious whole protein that some would call a miracle food. I wanted you to meet Don, because he was critical in making quinoa widely available.

TAL: You were the first guy to bring quinoa to the United States from South America. How did that happen?

DON: In the late '70s I was the ninth employee at a small company called Rockport Shoes. Production was in Brazil, so I found myself there and also in Bolivia and Chile. One of the things you experience when you're in South America and you're an American businessperson is people constantly coming up to you with things they would like to export—every day you're inundated with them, from strawberries to cars.

T: What made you specifically interested in quinoa?

D: It was the uniqueness of the food. I started importing some things from Bolivia, like fabrics, and in the back of my mind quinoa kept popping up. It seemed to me to have potential, because it looked like rice and could be cooked like rice but was really high in protein and iron. It wasn't so weird that you didn't know what to do with it, like teff or spelt. And it had sustained the Inca—a very poor people who barely ate any meat. Living at very high altitudes, they're living on quinoa. I was fascinated by that.

T: How did you learn about the nutrients back then?

D: There was some research conducted by the UNFAO [United Nations Food and Agriculture Organization] during World War II. That analysis showed that quinoa had a makeup similar to milk, and that intrigued me.

T: What made you think to bring it here?

D: Well, one day I was just sitting in my house in Boulder—this is 1980—and it's as if a lightbulb went on: I'm living at a high altitude, quinoa grows at a high altitude, and it occurs to me that quinoa could probably grow where I am.

T: So you decided to grow it yourself?

D: But I needed the seed. I called my friend Steve Gorad, who I'd known from the Arica Institute, a meditation group we'd both been involved with years before. He was married to a woman from Chile, and traveled there. I asked him if he could find some planting seed, which is different from the grain you eat. He managed to get a 100-kilo sack and arranged to get it to me.

T: Getting it here was tricky, you've said.

D: Sure. Here's this unknown package coming into the country from South America through Miami. It was poked probably a hundred times by people searching for something suspicious.

T: What happened with that first bag of seed?

D: Steve moved to Boulder around that time. We took some of the samples and planted them in our own backyards, and then we contacted an agronomist called Dwayne Johnson at Colorado State University. Dwayne was as fascinated with quinoa as we were. Once he was involved, the project gained credibility—we started planting in plots in the San Luis Valley. Steve found some of the [ancient Incan remnants of farms] down there that were still growing quinoa for themselves, and we started bringing in more seed from there.

T: So planting was working out?

D: We were having limited success. The varieties that we brought in from Bolivia were grown at even higher altitudes. So we thought, Let's try ten different altitudes and see what works. We were convincing farmers who were interested to commit a small plot. And CSU had a small plot too. And then a few other folks got involved along the way. Some of those plots panned out; most of them didn't.

"It seemed to me to have potential, because it looked like rice and could be cooked like rice. It wasn't so weird that you didn't know what to do with it."

T: But eventually you figured it out?

D: Yes, and by about 1982 we were bringing in planting seed by the container—20 metric tons at once. But marketing quinoa was another story. No one had any idea what to do with this stuff in 1981, '82. As luck would have it, Boulder had a couple of people in the grocery business. Pearl Street Market [later Alfalfa's, then Wild Oats, which was ultimately bought by Whole Foods] let us demo quinoa there, and we had people going gaga over this product. They just couldn't believe how good it was. High in protein, a complete protein—they weren't necessarily convinced about the nutritional value yet, but they thought it tasted great.

T: You still bring in the planting seeds from South America, right?

D: Right, because of day lengths, we need to import the seed from Bolivia. It's so close to the equator. We were able to pick up the altitude but we weren't able to pick up the latitude.

bibb lettuce, shaved fennel, *and* grapefruit salad *with* pickled onion

Bibb lettuce is delicate and makes a great base for stronger flavors. This is a simple winter salad that pairs tart grapefruit with sweet fennel and pickled onions—a mix that's both refreshing and piquant. This would be a nice starter for a hearty entrée.

For the onions:

1 red onion
1 cup white wine vinegar
¼ cup sugar
1 bay leaf

1 (1-inch) piece ginger, peeled and
   sliced paper thin
½ teaspoon red pepper flakes
2 teaspoons mustard seeds

For the vinaigrette:

1 pink grapefruit
1 tablespoon champagne vinegar
3 tablespoons extra-virgin olive oil
Sea salt and freshly ground
   black pepper

For the salad:

1 head Bibb lettuce, roughly chopped
1 fennel bulb, cut in half and thinly
   sliced on a mandoline

1   *Make the onions:* Cut the onion in half and thinly slice on a mandoline. Blanch in
    boiling water for 2 minutes, then chill in an ice bath. Place the remaining onion
    ingredients in a saucepan and bring to a boil. Simmer, covered, for 5 minutes. Add the
    onion, remove from the heat, and transfer to a glass container. Refrigerate for 1 hour,
    then drain and remove the bay leaf.

2   *Make the vinaigrette:* Cut the grapefruit into segments and set aside. Squeeze the
    juice from the grapefruit shells into a medium bowl and add the vinegar. Whisking
    constantly, slowly pour in the oil in a thin stream. Season with salt and pepper to taste.

3   *Assemble the salad:* Place the lettuce, fennel, grapefruit segments, and onion in a
    large bowl. Drizzle with the vinaigrette and toss to coat.

Makes 4 servings
Prep time: 20 minutes, plus 1 hour marinating

summer
chopped salad

This is super-easy—a foolproof recipe—but you should make it right before you serve it. Chopped salads can get soggy if they sit around. Kids go crazy for this because of all the great flavors and textures.

¼ pound green beans, cut into
   1-inch pieces
5 radishes, finely diced
Agave nectar
¼ English cucumber, finely diced
12 red and yellow cherry
   tomatoes, quartered
Kernels from 2 ears raw sweet corn

1 avocado, diced
1 cup baby arugula
1 shallot, minced
1 teaspoon minced fresh basil
1 teaspoon minced fresh oregano
Vinaigrette (recipe follows)
1 teaspoon freshly squeezed
   lemon juice

1   Blanch the green beans in boiling water for 30 seconds, then chill in an ice bath. In the same boiling water, blanch the radishes for 20 seconds, then chill in an ice bath sweetened with a touch of agave nectar.

2   Place all of the ingredients except for the Vinaigrette and lemon juice in a large bowl. Drizzle with the Vinaigrette and toss to coat. Sprinkle the lemon juice on top just before serving.

Makes 4 servings
Prep time: 20 minutes

✳ vinaigrette

1 tablespoon white wine vinegar
½ teaspoon agave nectar
3 tablespoons extra-virgin olive oil
Sea salt and freshly ground
   black pepper

Place the vinegar and agave nectar in a small bowl, then, whisking constantly, slowly pour in the oil in a thin stream. Season with salt and pepper to taste.

*

I love this at the end of the summer when you have the best corn of the season.

orange, belgian endive, *and* quinoa salad *with* champagne vinaigrette

This salad is rather elegant—perfect for a dinner party. I use champagne vinegar here because it's very delicate. The sweetness of the orange and the bitter taste of endive is a nice combination.

✳

The quinoa adds crunch to this sweet and bitter salad.

For the quinoa:

1 cup quinoa, cooked in vegetable
   stock according to package directions,
   cooled to room temperature
2 tablespoons finely diced red onion
1 tablespoon fresh basil chiffonade

¼ cup finely diced English cucumber
1 tablespoon extra-virgin olive oil
Sea salt and freshly ground black
   pepper to taste
Juice of 1 lemon

For the vinaigrette:

2 oranges
1 tablespoon champagne vinegar
3 tablespoons extra-virgin olive oil
Sea salt and freshly ground
   black pepper

To assemble:

Baby greens
1 head Belgian endive, leaves
   separated and trimmed into
   2-inch spears
Chives

1   *Make the quinoa:* Place all of the quinoa ingredients in a medium bowl and toss to combine.

2   *Make the vinaigrette:* Cut the oranges into segments; set aside. Squeeze 2 tablespoons juice from the orange shells into a small bowl. Add the vinegar and, whisking constantly, slowly pour in the oil in a thin stream until emulsified. Season with salt and pepper to taste.

3   *Assemble the salads:* Toss the baby greens with the vinaigrette to coat. Using tongs, divide the greens among 4 serving plates. Place 3 endive spears on top of the greens on each plate and fill with the quinoa mixture. Arrange the orange segments around the endive. Garnish with chives.

Makes 4 servings
Prep time: 20 minutes, not including quinoa cooking and cooling

*

This is just
a crisp,
fresh salad,
completely
improvised.

very green salad *with* cucumber, kohlrabi, sweet onion *and* herb vinaigrette

This salad is all about the dressing. I made it from leftovers at a friend's place in Hawaii, where there was an amazing herb garden. This particular dressing is very intense, and you barely cover the greens with it. If you have a sunny window, it's completely worthwhile to have a one-pot herb garden—grow your favorites in there, all together. Then you can mix up a dressing like this anytime.

1 garlic clove
1 small shallot
¼ cup loosely packed fresh parsley
1 small sprig fresh tarragon
3 fresh basil leaves
Needles from 1 sprig rosemary
3 tablespoons white wine vinegar
1 tablespoon light agave nectar
¼ teaspoon sea salt

¼ teaspoon freshly ground
  black pepper
2 teaspoons Dijon mustard
½ cup safflower oil
½ English cucumber, cut into
  ¼-inch-thick half-moons
2 heads romaine lettuce,
  roughly chopped
½ Vidalia onion, finely diced
1 kohlrabi, peeled and finely diced

1   In a food processor, mince the garlic and shallot. Scrape down the sides, then add the parsley, tarragon, basil, and rosemary. Pulse to chop.

2   Add the vinegar, agave nectar, salt, pepper, mustard, and 1 tablespoon water. Pulse again. With the machine running, slowly pour in the oil in a thin stream.

3   Place the cucumber, lettuce, onion, and kohlrabi in a large bowl. Drizzle with the vinaigrette and toss to coat.

Makes 4 servings
Prep time: 20 minutes

GUEST CHEF:
Scot Jones

"If you'd have asked me five years ago or even three years ago about cooking vegan, I'd have looked at you the way everyone looked at me— like I was crazy. The inspiration came from Tal: He showed me that you can take all the animal protein out and still be creative. It was like turning on a light. It's opened my mind as a chef. When people come to my table, they put their lives in my hands, literally. That's what I try to teach myself and my staff on a daily basis. Before VegiTerranean I was 45 pounds overweight. I had to take cholesterol medicine and heart medicine, but now all that's gone."

Scot and I were introduced by Chrissie Hynde, the lead singer of the Pretenders. Scot was running Fideli, a great Italian place that he still runs in Canton, Ohio, and he had never been exposed to vegan food. Chrissie wanted to open a vegetarian place in her hometown, and she went to Scot because, with its emphasis on fresh produce, Italian cooking lends itself so well to vegetarian preparations. I was brought in to help Scot get comfortable with vegetarian cooking. He got so comfortable, he decided to make the place vegan instead. And now, with incredibly flavorful, cozy dishes like biscuits and gravy (made with focaccia and morel mushroom gravy) and rutabaga pancakes, Scot's put his own stamp on vegan cooking and taken things to a new level.

Chef Scot Jones (right) with Chef Tal and Chrissie Hynde

MENU:

APPETIZER

Hot Italian Banana Peppers Stuffed with Fresh Herb Risotto and Soy Mozzarella, with Fresh Basil Lime Sauce

SALAD

Wild Field Green Salad with Sun-Dried Cherries and Blueberries, Fresh Strawberries, Sunflower Seeds, Tofu Ricotta, and a Warm Blueberry Vinaigrette

ENTRÉE

Gardein "Chicken" Piccata

Hot Italian Banana Peppers Stuffed with Fresh Herb Risotto and Soy Mozzarella, with Fresh Basil Lime Sauce

FOR THE RISOTTO:
1 cup olive oil
1 medium yellow onion, finely diced
8 cups Arborio rice
½ (750ml) bottle dry white wine
8 cups simmering water

FOR THE PEPPERS:
Spray oil
12 medium to large hot Italian
  banana peppers
2 cups Tofu Ricotta (page 83)
2 cups shredded soy mozzarella cheese,
  preferably Follow Your Heart brand
1 tablespoon minced shallot
1 tablespoon minced garlic
2 tablespoons chopped fresh basil
2 tablespoons chopped fresh parsley
2 tablespoons olive oil

FOR THE BASIL LIME SAUCE:
2 cups dry white wine
1 clove garlic, minced
1 tablespoon minced shallot
2 teaspoons sugar
2 tablespoons freshly squeezed
  lime juice
3 tablespoons chilled Earth
  Balance, cut into bits
1 cup chopped fresh basil

TO SERVE:
Chopped fresh basil
Chopped fresh parsley

Make the risotto:

Place a large pot over medium heat. Add the oil. When the oil is hot, add the onion and sauté until soft and translucent, 5 to 7 minutes. Add the rice and stir with a wooden spoon until the grains are opaque and very hot but not browned. Pour in the wine and stir until the liquid has been absorbed and the alcohol has evaporated. Add a ladleful of the simmering water and stir until absorbed. Add another ladleful of water and continue in this way, always waiting for the rice to absorb the liquid before adding more. After all the water has been added and the risotto is velvety and tender but the grains are still semi-firm to the bite, remove from the heat and let stand, stirring frequently, for 5 to 8 minutes, or until thickened.

Transfer the risotto to a baking sheet and spread out to cool for 1 hour. The risotto can be made in advance and kept, covered, in the refrigerator. Bring to room temperature before using.

NOTE:
*If you prefer less heat,
use mild Hungarian
wax peppers instead
of the Italian ones.*

Make the peppers:

Preheat the oven to 400°F. Spray a baking sheet with spray oil. Cut off the top of each pepper, leaving the top intact and setting it aside. Slit each pepper down the middle but not all the way through, and clean out the seeds. In a large bowl, combine the risotto, Tofu Ricotta, soy mozzarella, shallot, garlic, basil, and parsley. Gently stuff the peppers with the mixture; do not overstuff them, or they will cook unevenly.

Heat the oil in a large skillet over medium-high heat. Sauté the stuffed peppers until browned on the bottom, 3 to 5 minutes. Transfer to the baking sheet and bake for 10 minutes, or until heated through.

Make the basil lime sauce:

Pour off any excess oil from the skillet used to sauté the peppers. Place the skillet over medium-high heat and add the wine, garlic, shallot, sugar, and lime juice. Bring to a simmer and cook until the sauce is reduced by half, about 8 minutes. Remove from the heat and gradually stir in the Earth Balance, one piece at a time. Remove from the heat. When the sauce has cooled and thickened slightly, stir in the basil.

Assemble the dish:

Arrange the peppers on a serving platter, or place 2 peppers on each of 6 individual serving plates. Spoon the sauce over the peppers, garnish with basil and parsley, and serve immediately.

*Makes 6 servings
Prep time: 20 minutes*

Wild Field Green Salad with Sun-Dried Cherries and Blueberries, Fresh Strawberries, Sunflower Seeds, Tofu Ricotta, and a Warm Blueberry Vinaigrette

FOR THE VINAIGRETTE:
1 pint fresh blueberries
1 cup balsamic vinegar
1 teaspoon chopped garlic
1 teaspoon chopped shallot
1 cup light agave nectar
2 cups extra-virgin olive oil
Sea salt and freshly ground
   black pepper

NOTE:
You can use sun-dried cranberries in place of the cherries, if you wish, and use a few fresh blueberries in place of dried.

FOR THE TOFU RICOTTA:
1 pound firm tofu
½ teaspoon minced garlic
½ teaspoon minced shallot
½ teaspoon plum vinegar,
    preferably Umi brand (see note)
1 tablespoon freshly squeezed lemon juice

1 teaspoon extra-virgin olive oil
1 teaspoon nutritional yeast flakes
½ teaspoon chopped fresh basil
½ teaspoon chopped fresh parsley
Sea salt and freshly ground
    black pepper

FOR THE SALAD:
12 cups wild field greens or mesclun
Sea salt and freshly ground
    black pepper
¼ cup sun-dried cherries (see note)
¼ cup sun-dried blueberries
8 strawberries, sliced
3 tablespoons sunflower seeds,
    lightly toasted
6 teaspoons Tofu Ricotta

Make the vinaigrette:
In a food processor, combine the blueberries, vinegar, garlic, and shallot and pulse to chop. With the motor running, slowly add the agave nectar, then the oil. Season to taste with salt and pepper. The vinaigrette can be made up to 3 days in advance and kept, covered, in the refrigerator.

Make the Tofu Ricotta:
Press the tofu through a potato ricer into a large bowl. If you don't have a potato ricer, mash the tofu with your hands until crumbly. Add the remaining ingredients and mix well. It should be the consistency of ricotta cheese. **NOTE:** Plum vinegar can be found at natural foods stores.

Make the salad:
Put the greens in a large mixing bowl and season with salt and pepper. In a medium skillet, combine half of the vinaigrette, the cherries, blueberries, strawberries, and sunflower seeds. Cook over medium-high heat until heated through. Pour the mixture over the greens and toss well. Transfer to individual serving plates, making sure each plate gets some of all of the goodies, and top with Tofu Ricotta. Serve immediately.

Makes 6 servings
Prep time: 30 minutes

NOTE:

Be gentle with the Gardein breasts: Flatten them with your palm, not a mallet, being careful not to break them apart.

Gardein "Chicken" Piccata

6 (4-ounce) Gardein breasts, pressed thin
 and sliced on the bias
Sea salt and freshly ground black pepper
2 cups all-purpose flour
8 tablespoons Earth Balance
5 tablespoons extra-virgin olive oil
⅓ cup freshly squeezed lemon juice
½ cup vegan chicken or
 vegetable stock

½ cup dry white wine
¼ cup capers, rinsed
 and drained
½ teaspoon minced garlic
½ teaspoon chopped shallot
Pinch of sugar, if needed
⅓ cup chopped fresh parsley

Season the Gardein breasts with salt and pepper. Dredge in the flour and shake off the excess. In a large sauté pan over medium-high heat, melt 3 tablespoons of the Earth Balance with 3 tablespoons of the oil. When they start to sizzle, add 3 breasts and cook for 3 minutes, until browned on the bottom; flip and cook for another 3 minutes to brown the other side. Remove the breasts to a plate. Melt 2 more tablespoons of the Earth Balance with 2 tablespoons of the oil, heat until they sizzle, and cook the remaining 3 breasts in the same fashion. Remove the breasts to the plate.

Reduce the heat under the pan to medium-low and add the lemon juice, stock, wine, capers, garlic, and shallot. Bring to a boil, scraping up the browned bits from the pan for extra flavor. Check the seasoning and add more salt and pepper if needed. If the sauce is bitter, add the sugar.

Return the breasts to the pan and simmer for 3 to 5 minutes, until they are heated through and the sauce is thickened. Remove the breasts to a serving platter and add the remaining 3 tablespoons Earth Balance to the sauce. Whisk vigorously. Pour the sauce over the breasts and garnish with the parsley. Serve immediately, with sautéed spinach or braised escarole.

Makes 6 servings
Prep time: 45 minutes

Chapter

4

In winter, there's nothing cozier than having a pot of soup simmering on the stove. The house smells great, and you can stash extra soup in the freezer for another time. Many of the recipes in this section are really easy. The right garnish—one that makes sense flavor-wise as well as visually—dresses them up, making them as pretty as they are delicious.

corn chowder

Super-easy, hearty, and flavorful, this is a soup for peak corn season. It's a classic recipe, except the dairy is replaced with cashew cream. A lot of people use bacon in traditional corn chowder. I add chipotle pepper in my version for that same smokiness.

Sea salt

4 tablespoons extra-virgin olive oil

2 cups diced Vidalia onions

2 large carrots, peeled and cut into ¼-inch dice

1 celery stalk, cut into ¼-inch dice

1 red bell pepper, de-ribbed and cut into ¼-inch dice

1 dried chipotle pepper

5 cups faux chicken stock (try Better Than Bouillon brand)

2 large Yukon gold potatoes, peeled and cut into ¼-inch dice

2 fresh thyme sprigs

Kernels from 6 ears of corn, plus 2 ears roasted or grilled corn

1½ cups thick Cashew Cream (page 26)

Freshly ground black pepper

2 tablespoons minced chives

½ cup diced tomato

1   Place a large stockpot over medium heat. Sprinkle the bottom with a pinch of salt and heat for 1 minute. Add the oil and heat for 30 seconds, being careful not to let it smoke. This will create a nonstick effect.

2   Add the onions, carrots, celery, bell pepper, and chipotle pepper. Sauté for 10 minutes, stirring often. Add the stock, potatoes, and thyme, bring to a boil, reduce the heat, and simmer until the potatoes are tender, 15 to 20 minutes.

3   With the back of a spoon, smash some of the potatoes against the side of the pot and stir to thicken the soup. Add the raw corn and Cashew Cream, season with salt and pepper to taste, and simmer for 15 minutes. Remove the chipotle pepper and thyme sprigs. Garnish with the chives, tomato, and roasted corn kernels.

Makes 6 servings
Prep time: 1 hour

split pea soup
with tempeh bacon *and* chipotle cream

This is one of those soups that, eaten with a chunk of crusty baguette, is a whole meal in itself. Split pea is often made with ham. My version gets a double dose of smoky flavor from crispy tempeh bacon and chipotle cream. It's perfect for cold winter weather, and it makes the house smell great.

The smoky brown color of the soup comes from the roasted vegetable stock.

Sea salt
4 tablespoons Earth Balance
2 shallots, minced
2 leeks, thinly sliced
1 large carrot, coarsely chopped
3 cloves garlic, minced
1 teaspoon chopped fresh rosemary
1 bay leaf
1 teaspoon smoked paprika

5 cups vegetable stock or faux
  chicken stock (try Better Than
  Bouillon brand)
1½ cups green split peas, rinsed
Freshly ground black pepper
2 teaspoons canola oil
4 slices tempeh bacon
Chipotle Cream (recipe follows)

1   Place a large stockpot over medium heat. Sprinkle the bottom with a pinch of salt and
    heat for 1 minute. Add the Earth Balance and stir until melted, being careful not to let it
    burn. This will create a nonstick effect.

2   Add the shallots, leeks, carrot, and garlic and sauté for 5 minutes. Add the rosemary, bay
    leaf, and paprika and continue cooking for 2 minutes. Add the stock and split peas and
    season with salt and pepper to taste. Bring to a boil, then reduce the heat and simmer,
    uncovered, for 1 hour.

3   Meanwhile, heat the oil in a small skillet over medium-high heat. Add the tempeh bacon
    and fry on both sides until crisp. Cool, then coarsely crumble. Serve the soup garnished
    with the Chipotle Cream and tempeh bacon.

Makes 4 servings
Prep time: 1 hour, 15 minutes

✳ chipotle **cream**

¼ cup vegan mayonnaise
½ cup thick Cashew Cream (page 26)
½ canned chipotle in adobo sauce
Sea salt and freshly ground black pepper to taste
Juice of 1 lime

Place all of the ingredients in a food processor and blend until well mixed.

lemongrass consommé
with pea shoot and mushroom dumplings

This clean broth gets its kick from chiles, garlic, and ginger, making it intense but also delicate. The dumplings are surprisingly simple—you can use premade wonton wrappers, available at any Asian grocer. I like to serve this as a first course before an entrée of Thai noodles or coconut curry.

*

The dumplings are really easy and impressive.

For the consommé:

Sea salt
2 tablespoons canola oil
4 stalks lemongrass
2 stalks celery, diced
1 leek, thinly sliced
2 shallots, minced
1 (2-inch) piece fresh ginger,
   peeled and diced

3 cloves garlic, peeled and smashed
1 Kaffir lime leaf
2 small dried red chiles
1 teaspoon whole black peppercorns
2 tablespoons sugar
2 quarts vegetable or faux chicken stock
   (try Better Than Bouillon brand)

For the dumplings:

Sea salt
2 tablespoons canola oil
1 pound oyster mushrooms, minced
1 cup fresh pea shoots, minced
2 teaspoons minced fresh ginger
1½ teaspoons finely chopped chives

6 fresh basil leaves, chopped
1 tablespoon fresh parsley, minced
2 teaspoons shoyu soy sauce
Freshly ground black pepper
12 round wonton skins

To serve:

2 tablespoons thinly sliced scallion

1   *Make the consommé:* Place a large stockpot over medium heat. Sprinkle the bottom with
    a pinch of salt and heat for 1 minute. Add the oil and heat for 30 seconds, being careful
    not to let it smoke. This will create a nonstick effect. Add 1 teaspoon salt and all of the
    remaining ingredients except for the sugar and stock and sauté for 5 minutes, stirring
    frequently. Add the sugar and stock, bring to a boil, then reduce the heat and simmer for
    45 minutes.

2   *Make the dumplings:* Place a medium sauté pan over medium heat. Sprinkle the bottom
    with a pinch of salt and heat for 1 minute. Add the oil and heat for 30 seconds, being
    careful not to let it smoke. Add the mushrooms and sauté for 2 to 3 minutes, stirring
    occasionally, until they release their liquid. Add the pea shoots, ginger, chives, basil,
    parsley, and shoyu, season with salt and pepper to taste, and sauté for another 1 to 2
    minutes, until all the ingredients are combined and tender. Transfer to a bowl and cool.

3   Lay the wonton skins out on a clean, dry work surface. Put a small spoonful of the filling
    in the center of each. Using your finger or a brush, dab a bit of water around the edges
    of each wonton. Fold the wontons over the filling to create half-moons. Crimp the edges
    with your fingers, gathering them in little pinches. Pour the consommé through a fine-
    mesh sieve, discarding the solids, and return to the pot; bring to a simmer. Add the
    dumplings and heat for 10 minutes. Serve garnished with the scallion.

Makes 6 servings
Prep time: 1 hour

tomato bisque

The difference between bisque and other soups is that, in addition to being thick and pureed, a bisque showcases a single ingredient. I actually use canned tomatoes for this recipe.

Sea salt
4 tablespoons Earth Balance
1 onion, chopped
1 carrot, chopped
1 stalk celery, chopped
3 cloves garlic, smashed
2 tablespoons unbleached all-purpose flour
5 cups faux chicken stock (try Better Than Bouillon brand)

1 (28-ounce) can whole fire-roasted tomatoes, juice included
1 tablespoon minced fresh parsley
Leaves from 2 fresh thyme sprigs
1 bay leaf
Freshly ground black pepper
1½ cups regular Cashew Cream (page 26)
Parsley for garnish

1   Place a large stockpot over medium heat. Sprinkle the bottom with a pinch of salt and heat for 1 minute. Add the Earth Balance and stir until melted, being careful not to let it burn. This will create a nonstick effect. Add the onion, carrot, celery, and garlic and cook for 10 minutes, stirring frequently. Sprinkle the flour over the vegetables and continue cooking and stirring for 2 minutes.

2   Add the stock, tomatoes with juice, parsley, thyme, and bay leaf. Bring to a boil, then reduce the heat and simmer for 30 minutes. Season with salt and pepper, then add the Cashew Cream. Continue to simmer (do not boil) for 10 minutes.

3   Remove the bay leaf. Working in batches, pour the soup into a blender, cover the lid with a towel (the hot liquid tends to erupt), and blend on high for several minutes, until very smooth. Pour the soup through a fine-mesh sieve. Ladle into bowls and garnish with parsley.

Makes 6 servings
Prep time: 1 hour, 20 minutes

With a side of fresh-baked foccacia, this rich soup makes the perfect winter lunch.

cream *of*
asparagus soup

When I lived in Virginia, asparagus was one of the only locally fresh vegetables you could find in spring. This recipe is versatile: If you can't find nice asparagus, use broccoli to make cream of broccoli instead. As in a lot of my recipes, cashew cream stands in for dairy here and makes for an equally rich, delicious dish.

*

A simple micro-green garnish adds instant elegance.

Sea salt
3 tablespoons extra-virgin olive oil
1 large bunch asparagus, ends
   trimmed, cut into 2-inch pieces
2 stalks celery, chopped
1 large onion, chopped
2 quarts faux chicken or
   vegetable stock (try Better
   Than Bouillon brand)

1 bay leaf
1 cup thick Cashew Cream (page 26),
   plus more for garnish
Freshly ground black pepper
2 cups fresh baby spinach
Microgreens for garnish

1   Place a large stockpot over medium heat. Sprinkle the bottom with a pinch of salt and
     heat for 1 minute. Add the oil and heat for 30 seconds, being careful not to let it smoke.
     This will create a nonstick effect.

2   Add the asparagus, celery, and onion and sauté for 6 to 10 minutes, until the celery is
     just soft. Add the stock and bay leaf, bring to a boil, then reduce the heat and simmer for
     30 minutes. Add the Cashew Cream and simmer for an additional 10 minutes. Remove
     and discard the bay leaf. Season to taste with salt and pepper.

3   Working in batches, pour the soup into a blender, cover the lid with a towel (the hot
     liquid tends to erupt), and blend on high. Add the spinach to the last batch and continue
     blending until smooth. Pour the soup into a large bowl and stir to incorporate the
     spinach batch. Ladle into bowls. Garnish each bowl with microgreens and drops of
     Cashew Cream.

Makes 6 servings
Prep time: 1 hour, 15 minutes

my favorite
ROOT VEGETABLES

Roasting really brings out the flavor of root vegetables, whether you're making a big pot of winter soup or a crisp summer salad. Store roots in a cool, dark place for the longest life.

radishes They're great raw, but you can also blanch them in sugar water and then shock them with an ice bath—it takes the edge off but keeps them bright and crispy.

horseradish There's nothing like freshly grated horseradish in an aioli served with grilled shiitake mushrooms.

redskin potato Great piping hot, but I also like them in salads, where they're a little unexpected.

red onions Great with plum tomatoes in an Italian bread salad (panzanella).

ginger Indispensable for Asian sauces and dressings. When you shop for ginger, look for lighter-colored pieces, which are generally younger.

kohlrabi In flavor and texture, it's kind of a mix between a radish and an apple. It adds a nice crunch to salads.

parsnips I slice and deep-fry these for chips.

pearl onions Really nice in stews. They have a milder flavor than most onions. If you want to sauté them, blanch them first and the skins will come off easily.

beets You'll find these in many of my recipes, because I love them. I use them roasted, in salads, pickled, and more.

celery root soup *with* granny smith apples

This is the most popular soup I make—people go crazy for it. I first made it for a supper club I started at my friend Ko's jazz place in L.A. Throwing in some diced apples at the end adds a surprise tartness, and dots of chive oil give it a sleek, dramatic finish.

People can't believe this has no dairy, because it looks like a big bowl of heavy cream.

Sea salt
3 tablespoons extra-virgin olive oil
2 medium celery roots, peeled and cut
    into 1-inch cubes
2 stalks celery, chopped
1 large onion, chopped
2 quarts faux chicken or vegetable stock
    (try Better Than Bouillon brand)

1 bay leaf
1 cup thick Cashew Cream
    (page 26)
Freshly ground black pepper
1 Granny Smith apple, unpeeled,
    very finely diced
Chive Oil (recipe follows)

1   Place a large stockpot over medium heat. Sprinkle the bottom with a pinch of salt and heat for 1 minute. Add the oil and heat for 30 seconds, being careful not to let it smoke. This will create a nonstick effect.

2   Add the celery root, celery, and onion and sauté for 6 to 10 minutes, stirring often, until soft but not brown. Add the stock and bay leaf, bring to a boil, then reduce the heat and simmer for 30 minutes. Add the Cashew Cream and simmer for an additional 10 minutes.

3   Working in batches, pour the soup into a blender, cover the lid with a towel (the hot liquid tends to erupt), and blend on high. Season with salt and pepper to taste. Ladle into bowls. Place a spoonful of the diced apple in the center of each serving, drizzle the Chive Oil around the apple, and serve.

Makes 6 servings
Prep time: 1 hour, 10 minutes

✳ chive oil

1 small bunch chives
½ cup canola oil
Pinch of sea salt and freshly ground black pepper

Blanch the chives for 30 seconds in boiling water, then drain and chill in an ice bath. Drain, wrap the chives in a towel, and squeeze the moisture out. Place in a blender with the remaining ingredients and blend for 2 minutes. Strain through a fine-mesh sieve. Put the chive oil in a plastic squeeze bottle with a small opening or use a spoon for drizzling it on the soup.

Makes ½ cup

Chapter

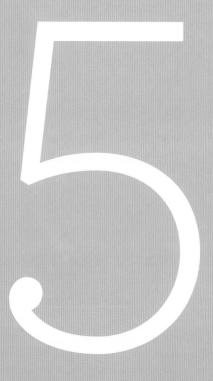

5

It's frustrating to order a vegetarian sandwich for lunch only to discover that it has no substance—just sprouts and roasted vegetables aren't enough. The sandwiches in this section are hearty—each of them contains a substantial protein—and really satisfying. They're meals in themselves.

SANDWICHES: Vietnamese-Style Tofu Hero with Asian Slaw (p104) *Gardein "Steak" Sandwich with Watercress, Red Pepper, and Horseradish Mayonnaise* (p106) Cajun Portobello Sandwich with Avocado and Rémoulade (p112) *Tomato, "Mozzarella," and Pesto Panini* (p116) California Gardein "Chicken" Salad (p118) *Herbed Cashew Cheese Baguette with Tomato and Watercress* (p120) Mediterranean Chickpea Wrap (p123) ✳

vietnamese-style
tofu hero *with* asian slaw

This hot sandwich is a little more complicated than some of the others but worth the time because it's so delicious. Based on a popular Vietnamese baguette sandwich called a báhn mi, it brings together sweet vegetables and spicy-savory tofu. The layering of flavors and textures makes it a sort of exotic comfort food.

For the tofu:

1 teaspoon freshly ground black pepper
¼ teaspoon white pepper
¼ teaspoon ground cayenne
½ teaspoon sweet paprika
1 teaspoon dry mustard

1 teaspoon ground ginger
¼ cup soy sauce
2 tablespoons minced chives
1 pound extra-firm tofu, cut into
   8 (¼-inch) slabs

To assemble:

4 French demi-baguettes, split
4 tablespoons vegan mayonnaise
4 tablespoons chile oil
4 fresh cilantro sprigs

½ English cucumber, cut
   lengthwise into 4 slices
Asian Slaw (recipe follows)

1   *Make the tofu:* Preheat the oven to 375°F. In a small bowl, whisk together all of the ingredients except for the tofu. Pour into a 9 by 13-inch baking dish. Place the tofu slabs in a single layer in the baking dish. Turn over to coat with the marinade. Bake for 20 minutes, turning the tofu over halfway through.

2   *Assemble the sandwiches:* Spread half of each baguette with 1 tablespoon of the mayonnaise and drizzle with 1 tablespoon of the chile oil. Layer 1 sprig of cilantro and 1 cucumber slice (cut to fit, if necessary).

3   Place two pieces of the tofu and a spoonful of the Asian Slaw on each baguette half. Top with remaining baguette halves and cut sandwiches in half. Serve immediately.

Makes 4 sandwiches
Prep time: 30 minutes

✳ asian **slaw**

2 tablespoons agave nectar
¼ cup rice vinegar
½ cup julienned carrot

½ cup julienned daikon radish
Sea salt and freshly ground black
   pepper to taste

Place all of the ingredients in a small bowl with ½ cup water and toss to combine. Store, covered, in the refrigerator for up to 2 days.

gardein "steak" sandwich
with watercress, red pepper, *and* horseradish mayonnaise

I've served this when I've had friends over to watch the World Cup, and for
college students in dining halls. It's always a winner—both hearty and satisfying.
If you have little children, make some extra Gardein strips and serve them as
"steak fingers" with a milder dipping sauce.

*Watercress adds a
peppery bite to this
meaty sandwich.*

For the steak strips:

8 ounces Gardein beef-style strips, thawed
3 tablespoons canola oil
1 tablespoon Steak Rub (recipe follows)

To assemble:

2 ciabattas or focaccia squares
Horseradish Mayonnaise (recipe follows)
¼ cup very thinly sliced red onion
½ cup chopped watercress
½ cup chopped romaine lettuce
½ red bell pepper, julienned

1   *Make the steak strips:* Using a dish towel or paper towel, rub each strip to remove the seasoning that comes on the packaged product. In a plastic bag or other container, toss the strips with the oil, then add the Steak Rub and toss again.

2   Place a cast-iron grill pan over medium-high heat. Sear the strips until lightly browned and heated through, 1 to 2 minutes on each side. Remove to a plate.

3   Cook the ciabattas on the grill pan, pressing down with a spatula, until toasted and grill-marked, turning over to toast both sides; split in half horizontally.

4   *Assemble the sandwiches:* Apply a generous amount of Horseradish Mayonnaise to the inside of each piece of ciabatta. Divide the onion, watercress, romaine, red pepper, and strips between the two bottom ciabatta pieces and cover with the top pieces. Serve immediately.

Makes 2 sandwiches
Prep time: 10 minutes

✳ steak **rub**

1½ tablespoons coarse sea salt
1 tablespoon freshly ground black pepper
1 tablespoon dehydrated onion
½ tablespoon dehydrated garlic

½ tablespoon red pepper flakes
½ tablespoon dried thyme
½ tablespoon dried rosemary
½ tablespoon dried fennel

Place all of the ingredients in a bowl and stir well to combine. Keeps for several months, tightly covered, in a cool, dark spot.

Makes 6 tablespoons

✳ horseradish **mayonnaise**

1 tablespoon prepared horseradish
1 cup vegan mayonnaise
1 teaspoon light agave nectar
Juice of 1 lemon

½ teaspoon sea salt
1 teaspoon freshly ground
   black pepper

Place all of the ingredients in a bowl and whisk well to combine. Store, covered, in the refrigerator for up to 2 weeks.

Makes 1 cup

THE MAYO MAN: Bob Goldberg

COFOUNDER OF FOLLOW YOUR HEART AND INVENTOR OF VEGENAISE, LOS ANGELES, CA

My friend Bob Goldberg is a quiet legend in the vegetarian community. He was one of the first to start a vegetarian café, back in the '70s, and then invented Vegenaise, the best mayo substitute I've ever had. Nowadays Bob's company, Follow Your Heart, has a completely solar-powered plant in L.A.— it actually sells electricity back to the city. He's always been a little ahead of the curve, and is a great inspiration for how a small business can grow and still maintain integrity.

 TAL: Take me back to the beginning. How did you get started?

BOB: Well, during the early 1970s, my friend Michael Besancon was operating a vegetarian food bar along with myself and two other friends. It was just a tiny concession in the back of a health food store in Canoga Park, initially only seven seats. It was definitely kind of strange, because the store itself wasn't vegetarian. Health food was considered strange back then, but vegetarian was really out there.

T: You were vegetarian, though.

B: I had just become vegetarian. I grew up in Chicago, the land of the stockyards. But I was going through major changes at this point. I had just gotten out of the army, and the whole idea of respect for life was very important to me. It transferred over to the food choices I made.

T: How did the café grow?

B: Somehow we got up to 22 seats—we just squeezed them in—and then we bought the store. We dumped all the meat out of there and made it a vegetarian place. That was a huge thing to do back then. We were advised not to, but what some people didn't understand was how valuable it was to vegetarians that they could come to a place where they could feel really safe about their food choices. Today in business, that's called "authenticity"—but at the time we were just following our hearts, and so that's what we named the store: Follow Your Heart.

T: You outgrew that location pretty quickly.

B: Yes, in 1976 we moved down the street to a place that used to be a butcher shop and neighborhood market—a 7,000-square-foot space. Kind of funny that we moved into a meat market. We went in there and steam-cleaned the place, and the fat in the walls was drawn out and dripped down to the floor, like the fat in a roasting pan. We did a massive cleaning. And there we set up a 49-seat restaurant. Today it's about 72. We're still in the same location.

T: Tell us how Vegenaise came to be.

B: Well, back in 1974 at the café, we weren't vegan but our policy was no meat, poultry, fish, or eggs. So on sandwiches, instead of mayonnaise, we were using this product called Lecinaise that was not supposed to have any eggs in it. But then one day it came out that Lecinaise was a total fraud. This guy was busted in the middle of the night soaking labels off a cheap brand of supermarket mayonnaise and slapping his label on there. This was a huge problem for us at the restaurant, because Lecinaise tasted great and our sandwiches depended on it. And so we did lots of research into making mayo without eggs.

T: And you figured it out.

B: This is freaky, but I had a dream about how to solve the problem. I sat bolt upright in bed. The next morning I tried it and it worked. That's when we started making the product. We didn't have a facility yet, so went around to some companies and had them produce it for us. They didn't understand the ingredients we used—the very early version was made with tofu scraps that we got from a tofu factory—and the quality control wasn't good. We only wanted small quantities, so we were just a bother to these manufacturers. And the product didn't keep very well unless we refrigerated it. And everybody knows that mayo is found on the dry shelf in the supermarket, so we could never figure out what to do with it.

T: **What changed that for you?**

B: Well, people wanted it so badly they were buying it from us at the restaurant and taking it home in paper cups. So we thought, How bad could it be to try to sell it from the refrigerated section of the grocery store? We'll just see what happens. It turned out to be a good move. Since we could refrigerate it, we didn't have to compromise the formula—it tasted like the day we made it. People were happy. We still make it the same today, at our own facility.

"What some people didn't understand was how valuable it was to vegetarians that they could come to a place where they could feel really safe about their food choices."

T: **And your plant is all solar-powered.**

B: Yes. In L.A. it's not hard to be solar-powered—it's expensive as hell, but back in 2003, when we made the plant solar, the rebates were really high. Today it's not as generous an environment. But from the beginning, our power usage was less than the power we could generate—and the photovoltaic panels last forever, at least 50 years.

T: **The restaurant is still thriving after all this time.**

B: It's a very magical place. Now the people doing the cooking are second generation—the kids of those of us who started it or of people who worked there or of customers. They grew up there and they love it. It's sort of self-sustaining. It's kind of funny—my daughter always thought it was a little weird. She never made much of a deal that her family was involved with the store until she got into high school and some of her friends and teachers realized her connection. And then she suddenly discovered how cool it was.

cajun portobello sandwich
with avocado *and* rémoulade

Marinating mushrooms takes out a bit of the earthy flavor that some people find off-putting. Of course, the longer they marinate, the more intensity you'll get. This is a rich sandwich, with luscious avocado and a generous smear of rémoulade (which also makes a perfect dip for steamed artichokes).

For the mushrooms:

Sea salt
¼ cup extra-virgin olive oil
2 shallots, chopped
2 garlic cloves, minced
2 to 3 tablespoons low-salt
   Cajun seasoning
½ cup dry white wine
1½ tablespoons white wine
   vinegar
4 large portobello mushrooms,
   stemmed, gills removed, cut on
   the bias into ¼-inch slices

To assemble:

About ¼ cup Rémoulade (recipe follows)
4 soft sandwich rolls, split
4 to 8 romaine lettuce leaves,
   rinsed and dried
1 large tomato, thinly sliced
1 ripe avocado, peeled, pit removed,
   and sliced

1   *Make the mushrooms:* Place a large pot over medium heat. Sprinkle the bottom with a pinch of salt and heat for 1 minute. Add the oil and heat for 1 minute, being careful not to let it smoke. This will create a nonstick effect.

2   Add the shallots and garlic and cook for 3 to 4 minutes, until softened. Add 1 tablespoon of the Cajun seasoning, along with the wine, vinegar, and 1 cup water, bring to a boil, then lower the heat and simmer for 20 minutes.

3   Add the mushrooms and cook for 1 minute. Pour the mushrooms and liquid into a shallow container, cover, and set aside to marinate for 1 hour.

4   Remove the mushrooms from the marinade and press between paper towels or in a cotton dish towel to remove the excess marinade, then sprinkle with the remaining Cajun seasoning, pressing the seasoning into both sides of the mushroom slices. Discard the marinade.

5   In a cast-iron skillet over medium-high heat, cook the mushrooms in a single layer (you may have to do this in two batches) until blackened, 2 to 3 minutes on each side. Remove to a plate.

6   *Assemble the sandwiches:* Spread a spoonful of the Rémoulade on one half of each roll. Top each with 1 or 2 lettuce leaves and a few slices of tomato and avocado. Divide the mushroom slices among the rolls. Close each sandwich, cut in half, and serve.

Makes 4 sandwiches
Prep time: 30 minutes, plus 1 hour marinating

rémoulade

1 cup vegan mayonnaise
1 tablespoon ketchup
1 tablespoon Dijon mustard
1 teaspoon hot sauce
1 teaspoon vegan Worcestershire sauce
1 tablespoon freshly squeezed
   lemon juice

¼ teaspoon sea salt
2 teaspoons capers, minced
2 teaspoons minced shallot
1 teaspoon minced fresh parsley
2 teaspoons minced red
   bell pepper

Place all the ingredients in a food processor or blender and blend on high for 1 minute. Store, covered, in the refrigerator for up to 1 week.

Makes 1¼ cups

my favorite
PICKLED THINGS

I love pickled vegetables as condiments—they're great for bringing a salty, pungent flavor to the plate, or as a garnish to add crunch. Most store-bought brands have additives (many of the Japanese pickles you'll find on the shelves have MSG). But it's fun and easy to make your own— a nice weekend activity. You can do it seasonally with whatever you find at the green market, and it's a great way to use up leftovers in your vegetable drawer. Here's what to do: Using a 4-to-1 ratio (you'll want enough liquid to cover the cut vegetables completely), bring white wine vinegar and sugar, plus whatever seasonings you like (red pepper flakes, mustard seed, etc.) to a boil in a saucepan. Simmer, covered, for 5 minutes, then add your cut vegetables and remove the pan from the heat. Transfer everything to a glass container and refrigerate for 1 hour. Drain and serve, or save covered in the refrigerator for up to 1 month.

cabbage (sauerkraut)

ginger

turnips

green tomato

garlic

tomato, "mozzarella," *and* pesto **panini**

Traditional pesto is made with basil, but you can use all sorts of different greens. Here I make a pesto from peppery arugula to give a kick to a classic combo— vegan mozzarella and tomato. Double your batch and stash some pesto in the fridge so that you can toss it with pasta later in the week.

*

If you don't have a panini press, you can make do with a couple of cast-iron skillets.

For the pesto:

¼ cup pine nuts
3 cloves garlic, minced
2 cups coarsely chopped arugula,
    stems included
¼ cup coarsely chopped fresh basil

2 tablespoons nutritional yeast flakes
Sea salt and freshly ground
    black pepper to taste
Pinch of ground cayenne
½ cup extra-virgin olive oil

To assemble:

½ loaf plain focaccia or other bread
1 large tomato, thinly sliced
4 slices vegan mozzarella
4 teaspoons olive oil

1   *Make the pesto:* Place all of the pesto ingredients except the oil in a food processor and pulse several times. Continue to blend as you slowly pour in the oil in a thin stream.

2   *Assemble the sandwiches:* Cut the focaccia into 4 equal-sized pieces. Split each piece in half horizontally. Spread one of the halves of each split piece of focaccia with about ¼ of the pesto. Divide the tomato and mozzarella slices among the sandwiches. Drizzle each with 1 teaspoon oil and close the sandwiches.

3   Cook the sandwiches one at a time in a panini press set on medium-high until the cheese is melted and the bread is golden, about 3 minutes. Alternatively, preheat two cast-iron skillets over medium-high heat; put a sandwich in one hot skillet and carefully set the second one on top to press the sandwich. Flip the panini halfway through. Serve immediately.

Makes 4 sandwiches
Prep time: 15 minutes

california gardein "chicken" salad

It's so easy, and everyone loves this old-fashioned (vegan) chicken salad with some champagne grapes tossed in for sweetness and color. Toasted walnuts bring crunch, richness, and extra protein. The dressing is unique thanks to the lime, and agave nectar adds a summery sweetness as well.

1 cup vegan mayonnaise
2 teaspoons rice vinegar
Juice of 1 lime
1 tablespoon agave nectar
2 pounds Gardein chicken-style
   strips, thawed and coarsely pulsed
   in a food processor or chopped
   by hand

¾ cup walnuts, toasted and
   coarsely chopped
1 cup champagne grapes
3 stalks celery, diced ¼ inch
Sea salt and freshly ground
   black pepper to taste

Place all of the ingredients in a large bowl and toss gently to combine. Serve on your bread of choice.

Makes 8 servings
Prep time: 10 minutes

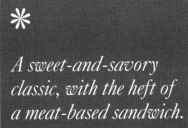

herbed cashew cheese baguette *with* tomato and watercress

One ingredient here that you might not be familiar with is probiotic powder—you can find it with the refrigerated vitamins at places like Whole Foods. Probiotics help culture cheese and give it its sharp flavor. Once you try the process, you'll see that making cashew cheese isn't tough at all (though it does take some time). You can double the cheese recipe here and store the extra in the refrigerator for up to two weeks—I recommend it. Everyone loves this cheese, and it tends to disappear.

This cashew cheese is the invention of my friend Chad, a raw food genius.

2 cups whole raw cashews
1 teaspoon New Chapter All-Flora
    probiotic (use the powder from
    6 capsules)
1 tablespoon onion powder
½ teaspoon white pepper

1 tablespoon nutritional yeast flakes
1 teaspoon sea salt
Pinch of freshly grated nutmeg
2 tablespoons chopped fresh tarragon
2 tablespoons chopped fresh chives
Freshly ground black pepper

To assemble:

1 cup watercress
2 French baguettes, split lengthwise
    and cut in half crosswise
4 large Roma tomatoes, sliced ¼ inch thick
2 tablespoons extra-virgin olive oil
Sea salt and freshly ground black pepper

1   *Make the cashew cheese:* Put the cashews in a bowl and add cold water to cover them.
     Cover the bowl and refrigerate for 12 to 14 hours.

2   In a cup, combine the probiotic powder with 2 tablespoons water and stir until smooth.
     Place the nuts in a blender with the probiotic mixture. Blend on high for several minutes,
     stopping to scrape the sides with a rubber spatula, until very smooth. Line a fine-mesh
     sieve with three layers of rinsed and squeezed cheesecloth, leaving plenty of overhang,
     and set over a bowl. Transfer the nut mixture to the sieve and fold the excess cheesecloth
     over the top, twisting to ensure it is tight. Place heavy cans or a gallon jug of water on
     top of the cheese and set in a warm place for 14 to 16 hours to culture. Transfer the cheese
     to a medium bowl.

3   Stir in the onion powder, white pepper, nutritional yeast, salt, and nutmeg. Scoop the
     cheese culture into the center of a sheet of parchment paper. Roll into a 2-inch-diameter
     log and refrigerate for several hours or overnight until firm.

4   Combine the herbs and pepper to taste on a plate, then unwrap the cheese log and roll
     in the mixture to coat. Cut into ¼-inch slices.

5   *Assemble the sandwiches:* Arrange the watercress over the bottom halves of the
     baguettes. Top with the tomato slices, drizzle with the oil, and season with salt and
     pepper to taste. Arrange the cheese slices over the tomatoes and cover with the top
     halves of the baguettes. Serve immediately.

Makes 4 sandwiches
Prep time: 20 minutes, plus 2 days soaking and culturing (but worth it)

mediterranean
chickpea wrap

Here's a take on a sandwich by my friend Greg Peterman, in Virginia. He owns
a terrific deli that's half vegetarian, half regular. This is a great mash-up of strong
ingredients—chickpeas, sun-dried tomatoes, cumin, onions, and lots of garlic.
When Greg does this wrap, he includes vegetarian sausage, so that's something you
might want to throw in there. With or without, it's one of my favorite sandwiches.

Sea salt
2 tablespoons olive oil
1 carrot, peeled and finely diced
1 onion, finely diced
1 banana pepper, seeded and finely diced
1 garlic clove, minced
1 teaspoon ground cumin
½ teaspoon red pepper flakes
⅛ teaspoon ground cayenne, or
  more to taste

Freshly ground black pepper
1 (15-ounce) can chickpeas,
  with liquid
1 white potato, peeled and finely diced
5 whole oil-packed sun-dried tomatoes,
  coarsely chopped
4 pieces vegan naan bread or tortillas,
  heated or toasted

1   Place a large sauté pan over medium heat. Sprinkle the bottom with a pinch of salt
    and heat for 1 minute. Add the oil and heat for 1 minute, being careful not to let
    it smoke. This will create a nonstick effect.

2   Add the carrot, onion, banana pepper, and garlic to the pan and sauté, stirring
    frequently, for 5 to 7 minutes, until the vegetables are just beginning to soften. Add
    the cumin, red pepper, cayenne, and black pepper to taste and sauté for 1 minute.

3   Add the chickpeas and their liquid and 1½ cups water. Bring to a boil. Add the potato
    and sun-dried tomatoes and simmer for 20 minutes, or until the potatoes are soft.
    Serve wrapped in the naan bread or tortillas.

Makes 4 sandwiches
Prep time: 45 minutes

Chef Profile

RESTAURANT:
Saf, London's first full
vegan restaurant and bar

SPECIALTY:
Haute raw

PERSONAL ORIENTATION:
Raw vegan

GUEST CHEF:
Chad Sarno

✳ *"As a child, I was blessed with asthma—blessed in that it brought me to where I am today. I was involved in sports but always sitting out because I had so many asthma attacks. At a certain point, I was going to the hospital every Saturday morning to breathe out of some tank. I was on all sorts of different inhalers. A friend of the family told me he'd heard that if you stopped eating dairy products, it would help your asthma. I was never a big meat-eater—I ate a lot of seafood and dairy, though. I'd have ice cream before bed and then I'd cough all night. But as soon as I stopped eating dairy, my asthma went away. I immediately stopped using all inhalers. I was about 17 at the time, and I've never experienced asthma since. That's what sparked my interest in health."*

I never took raw food seriously until I met Chad. There were always a couple of raw recipes on the menu at the restaurants where I worked, and they were a pain. I'd think, This is fine until you get to the point of dehydrating—and at that step I'd want to throw it in the deep fryer. But Chad really turned me around. When he was setting up his restaurant Saf in London (now a huge success), he asked me to help with the opening, and that really altered my perspective. I saw a full working raw kitchen, instead of the stuff I was used to. There was a whole line of dehydrators instead of convection ovens. One of the most amazing things is Chad's Cashew Cheese, which is made using the same process as dairy cheese. It is just fantastic.

Chef Chad Sarno with Chef Tal

CHAD'S
MENU:

SALAD

Macadamia Caprese

APPETIZER

Beet Ravioli with Balsamic Pickled Figs and
Green Garlic Oil

ENTRÉE

Wild Mushroom Farinata with Artichoke Aioli and
Roasted Cherry Tomatoes

Macadamia Caprese

FOR THE MACADAMIA CHEESE:

2 cups macadamia nuts

1 teaspoon New Chapter All-Flora probiotic
(use the powder from 6 capsules), or any
other probiotic powder of comparable
quality, dissolved in 1 cup warm water

2 tablespoons nutritional yeast flakes (optional)

1 tablespoon onion powder

½ teaspoon white pepper

Pinch of freshly grated nutmeg

1 teaspoon sea salt

¼ cup chopped fresh tarragon

3 tablespoons chopped fresh chives

1½ teaspoons freshly ground black pepper

FOR THE SEMI-DRIED TOMATOES:

6 to 8 vine-ripened tomatoes on the stem

Cajun spice mix, or red pepper flakes

Coarse sea salt

TO SERVE:

2 cups baby mizuna or baby spicy
greens mix

1 tablespoon extra-virgin olive oil or
Green Garlic Oil (page 128), plus more
for drizzling

Coarse Maine smoked sea salt
(hickory- or apple-smoked)

Make the macadamia cheese:
Put the macadamia nuts in a bowl and add cold water to cover them. Cover the bowl and refrigerate for 12 to 14 hours. Drain and rinse the nuts under warm water.

Place the nuts in a blender with the probiotic mixture. Blend on high for several minutes, stopping to scrape the sides with a rubber spatula, until very smooth. Line a fine-mesh sieve with three layers of rinsed and squeezed cheesecloth, leaving plenty of overhang, and set over a bowl. Transfer the nut mixture to the sieve and fold the excess cheesecloth over the top, twisting to ensure it is tight. Place heavy cans or a gallon jug of water on top of the cheese and set in a warm place for 14 to 16 hours to culture.

Transfer the cheese to a medium bowl and stir in the nutritional yeast (if using), onion powder, white pepper, nutmeg, and salt. On a work surface, combine the tarragon, chives, and black pepper. On a piece of plastic wrap, form the cheese into a log, then roll the log in the herb mixture to cover the entire surface. Set aside.

Make the semi-dried tomatoes:
Cut a small X in the bottom of each tomato and put in a large bowl. Pour hot (not boiling) water over the tomatoes, being careful not to break the stems. Cover the bowl and let the tomatoes sit for 10 minutes, then use a slotted spoon to gently remove them to an ice bath to chill. Carefully peel off the skin, making sure the stems are not removed.

Place the tomatoes on a screen; sprinkle the top of each tomato with the Cajun spice mix and salt to taste. Let them sit for 4 to 6 hours, until the outsides of the tomatoes are a bit firm.

Assemble the salad:
Gently slice the cheese roll to make 3 slices per serving. Cut the tomatoes in half. Toss the greens with some of the oil. On each of 6 to 8 small rectangular serving plates, place a small pile of the greens on one end. Divide the cheese slices and tomato halves among the plates, arranging them in a row, alternating and overlapping them slightly. Sprinkle with smoked salt and drizzle with additional oil. Serve immediately.

Makes 6 to 8 servings
Prep time: 20 minutes, plus 2 days soaking and culturing

Beet Ravioli with Balsamic Pickled Figs and Green Garlic Oil

FOR THE GREEN GARLIC OIL:
1 cup chopped fresh chives
½ cup chopped fresh parsley
Pinch of sea salt
2 cups grapeseed oil or mild olive oil
3 tablespoons coarsely chopped young garlic

FOR THE PICKLED FIGS:
2 cups small dried figs
4 sprigs fresh thyme
Pinch of coarse sea salt
1 cup balsamic vinegar

FOR THE BEETS:
2 large beets
Sea salt and freshly ground black
pepper
1 bunch asparagus spears, shaved
    with a vegetable peeler
1 tablespoon toasted pumpkin
    seed oil
1 tablespoon minced fresh chives
Coarse sea salt
Freshly cracked black pepper

FOR THE CASHEW CHEESE:
2 cups whole raw cashews
1 teaspoon New Chapter All-Flora
    probiotic (use the powder from
    6 capsules), or any other probiotic
    powder of comparable quality,
    dissolved in 1 cup warm water
2 tablespoons nutritional yeast flakes
½ tablespoon onion powder
1½ tablespoons minced fresh chives
2 tablespoons minced fresh parsley
2 tablespoons minced shallot
1 teaspoon sea salt
Freshly ground black pepper to taste

Make the green garlic oil:
In a blender, combine the chives, parsley, salt, and oil and blend until very smooth. Pour the mixture through a fine-mesh sieve set over a bowl, stirring gently to allow the oil to flow through. Discard the solids. Add the garlic to the oil and set aside to infuse at room temperature for 1 day.

Make the pickled figs:
Put the figs, thyme, and salt in a nonreactive bowl or large jar and cover with the vinegar. Set aside to macerate at room temperature for 1 day.

NOTE:
This recipe needs to be started a day in advance, but requires very little last-minute preparation.

Make the cashew cheese:

Put the cashews in a bowl and add cold water to cover them. Cover the bowl and refrigerate for 12 to 14 hours. Drain and rinse the cashews under warm water.

Place the nuts in a blender with the probiotic mixture. Blend on high for several minutes, until very smooth. Transfer to a clean glass bowl, cover with cheesecloth, and set in a warm place for 14 to 16 hours to culture.

Transfer to a medium bowl and stir in the remaining ingredients. Scoop ½ cup of the cheese into a pastry bag. (Leftover cashew cheese will keep, covered, in the refrigerator for up to 1 week.)

Make the beets:

Peel the beets and use a mandoline or a very sharp knife to slice them paper thin. Gently toss the slices with a drizzle of green garlic oil and sprinkle with salt and pepper to taste. Let marinate for 1 hour.

Place a slice of beet on a work surface and mound 1 tablespoon of the cashew cheese in the center. Cover with a second beet slice. Repeat with the remaining beet slices and cheese. Arrange 6 ravioli in the center of each serving plate.

In a small bowl, toss the asparagus with the pumpkin seed oil and divide among the plates, piling in the center of the ravioli. Scatter the pickled figs and chives over the plates, drizzle with green garlic oil, and sprinkle with salt and pepper. Serve immediately.

Makes 6 to 8 servings
Prep time: 20 minutes, plus 1 day for pickling and culturing

Wild Mushroom Farinata with Artichoke Aioli and Roasted Cherry Tomatoes

FOR THE FARINATA BATTER:
¾ to 1 cup olive oil
1 tablespoon sea salt
1½ to 2 cups chickpea flour
    (besan, or gram flour)
2 tablespoons chopped fresh rosemary

FOR THE ARTICHOKE AIOLI:
1 cup whole raw cashews
½ cup plain soy milk
2 garlic cloves
¼ cup maple syrup
3 tablespoons brown rice vinegar
¼ cup olive oil
Sea salt
2 tablespoons minced fresh chives
1½ tablespoons minced fresh tarragon
¼ cup coarsely chopped artichoke hearts
3 tablespoons capers, drained

FOR THE ROASTED TOMATOES:
8 ounces cherry tomatoes on the vine
3 sprigs fresh thyme
Olive oil
Sea salt and freshly ground black pepper

FOR THE MUSHROOMS:
Sea salt
2 tablespoons Earth Balance
1½ cups loosely packed wild mushrooms,
    preferably chanterelles
2 garlic cloves, minced
2 tablespoons minced fresh chives
Freshly ground black pepper

TO COOK AND SERVE:
2 tablespoons Earth Balance
8 ounces (1½ cups) pine nuts, toasted
2 tablespoons minced fresh parsley

Make the farinata batter:
In a blender, combine 3 cups warm water with the oil, salt, 1½ cups chickpea flour, and the rosemary and blend until smooth. Add more flour if necessary to make the mixture the consistency of pancake batter. Set aside.

Make the artichoke aioli:
In a clean blender, combine the cashews, soy milk, garlic, maple syrup, vinegar, and oil and blend until smooth. Season with salt to taste. Transfer to a medium bowl and stir in the chives, tarragon, artichoke hearts, and capers. Set aside.

Make the roasted tomatoes:
Preheat the oven to 250°F. Put the tomatoes and thyme in a baking dish and drizzle with a bit of oil. Season with salt and pepper to taste and toss to lightly coat. Roast for about 10 minutes, until the tomato skins crack.

Make the mushrooms:
Place a large sauté pan over medium heat. Sprinkle the bottom with a pinch of salt and heat for 1 minute. Add the Earth Balance and stir until melted, being careful not to let it burn. This will create a nonstick effect. Add the mushrooms and garlic and sauté until the mushrooms have released their liquid and the pan is almost dry, about 4 minutes. Gently stir in the chives, season with salt and pepper to taste, and remove from the heat.

Cook and serve:
Place a crêpe pan or griddle over medium heat and add enough Earth Balance to lightly coat the bottom. Ladle about 1 cup of the batter onto the center of the pan. Cook until golden brown on the bottom, about 3 to 4 minutes, then flip it over and brown the other side. Remove to a plate and cover to keep warm while you make the remaining crêpes, using more Earth Balance as necessary.

Cover half of each crêpe with some of the mushrooms, drizzle with the aioli, then fold closed. Garnish with another dollop of aioli, some roasted tomatoes, a few pine nuts, and parsley. Serve immediately.

Makes 6 crêpes
Prep time: 20 to 25 minutes

Chapter

The reason a lot of people don't feel full when they eat a vegetarian meal, even at a top restaurant, is that they're missing the protein— every course is just vegetables. But that's easy to address. All the entrées here—from the quickest dish to the most elaborate—revolve around a center-of-the-plate plant-based protein. Each one's an example of how satisfying vegan food can be.

ENTRÉES: Pine-Nut-and-Basil Seared Gardein "Chicken" with Lobster Mushroom Beurre Blanc, Braised Kale, and Roasted Fingerling Potatoes(p134) *Old Bay Tofu Cakes with Pan-Roasted Summer Vegetables, Horseradish Cream, Apples, and Beets(p138)* Peppercorn-Encrusted Portobello Fillets with Yellow Tomato Béarnaise and Mashed Potatoes(p142) *Free-Form Ravioli with Tofu Ricotta and Arugula Pesto(p146)* Tempeh Creole over Brown Rice(p150) *Gardein "Chicken" Scaloppini with Shiitake Sake Sauce, Braised Pea Shoots, and Crispy Udon Noodle Cakes(p154)* Paella with "Sausage," Nori-Dusted Oyster Mushrooms, and Wine-Braised Artichoke Hearts(p160) *Artichoke Ricotta Tortellini with Saffron Cream Sauce(p164)* Agave-Lime Grilled Tofu with Asian Slaw and Mashed Sweet Potatoes(p178) *Whole Wheat Penne with San Marzano Tomatoes(p184)* Asparagus and Meyer Lemon Risotto(p186) *Cornmeal-Crusted Tempeh with Smoked Tomato Sauce, Green Chile Relish, Black Bean Puree, and Braised Kale(p190)* ✳

pine-nut-*and*-basil seared gardein "chicken" *with* lobster mushroom beurre blanc, braised kale, *and* roasted fingerling potatoes

✳ *The toasted pine nut crust adds crunch and flavor.*

This dish uses Gardein "chicken," a great tasting and high-protein product that is a great transitional option for people new to vegetarian cuisine. You can find it in the frozen and fresh sections of your local grocery store. Kale cuts the richness of the sauce and the "meat" just enough.

For the chicken:

1 cup pine nuts, toasted
1 cup unbleached all-purpose flour
5 large basil leaves, cut into chiffonade
4 Gardein breasts, thawed

Sea salt and freshly ground
    black pepper
4 tablespoons canola oil

For the lobster mushroom beurre blanc:

Sea salt
1 teaspoon extra-virgin olive oil
2 shallots, minced
1 pound lobster mushrooms,
    cut into brunoise
½ cup dry white wine
½ cup regular Cashew Cream (page 26)
2 tablespoons nutritional yeast flakes
8 tablespoons Earth Balance, cut into
    tablespoon-sized pieces
Juice of 1 lemon
1 tablespoon minced fresh chives
Freshly ground black pepper

ABOUT GARDEIN:
Gardein, the protein in this recipe, looks and tastes like chicken but contains no animal or dairy ingredients. It has a savory taste and authentic texture and is made from a blend of vegetables and grains—soy, wheat, ancient grains, peas, beets, and carrots, among others. Gardein was created by my friend Yves Potvin (read about him on page 157). I've been fortunate enough to chime in on the product development, helping out with flavors, textures, new variations, and uses.

To serve:

Braised Kale (recipe follows)
Roasted Fingerling Potatoes
    (recipe follows)

✳ braised **kale**

Sea salt
2 tablespoons extra-virgin olive oil
1½ pounds kale, stems removed,
   roughly chopped

½ cup vegetable stock
Freshly ground black pepper
1 tablespoon Earth Balance

Place a large sauté pan over medium heat. Sprinkle the bottom with a pinch
of salt and heat for 1 minute. Add the oil and heat for 30 seconds, being careful
not to let it smoke. This will create a nonstick effect.

   Add the kale and sauté for 3 to 4 minutes, stirring frequently, until wilted.
Add the stock, season with salt and pepper to taste, and cook for 5 minutes.

   Remove from the heat and stir in the Earth Balance. Drain the excess liquid.
Serve immediately.

Makes about 2 cups

✳ roasted **fingerling potatoes**

1 pound fingerling potatoes, washed and thoroughly dried
2 tablespoons extra-virgin olive oil
1 tablespoon fresh thyme leaves
Sea salt and freshly ground black pepper to taste

Preheat the oven to 450°F. In a bowl, toss the potatoes with the rest of
the ingredients. Transfer to a baking sheet and spread in a single layer.
Bake until crisp on the outside and tender on the inside, about 25 minutes.
Serve warm.

Makes 1 pound

1   *Make the chicken:* Preheat the oven to 200°F. In a food processor, pulse the pine nuts, flour, and basil. Transfer to a shallow bowl or plate.

2   Flatten the breasts with your hand to ½ inch thick. Season each side with salt and pepper to taste, then press each side into the pine nut dredge.

3   Place a large sauté pan over medium heat. Sprinkle the bottom with a pinch of salt and heat for 1 minute. Add the oil and heat for 30 seconds, being careful not to let it smoke. This will create a nonstick effect.

"Gardein has the bite and texture of real meat—most people can't tell it from the real thing."

4   Place the breasts in the pan and cook until golden brown, about 2 minutes on each side. Remove to a wire rack set over a paper-towel-lined baking sheet and put in the oven to keep warm while you make the sauce.

5   *Make the lobster mushroom beurre blanc:* Place a medium sauté pan over medium heat. Sprinkle the bottom with a pinch of salt and heat for 1 minute. Add the oil and heat for 30 seconds, being careful not to let it smoke.

6   Reduce the heat to low. Add the shallots and sauté until translucent but not browned, 2 to 3 minutes. Add the mushrooms and sauté for 2 minutes. Add the wine and cook until reduced by half. Add the Cashew Cream and continue to cook for 5 minutes, then whisk in the nutritional yeast.

7   Remove from the heat. Whisk in the Earth Balance 1 tablespoon at a time, then stir in the lemon juice and chives. Season with salt and pepper to taste.

8   *Assemble the dish:* Place portions of the Braised Kale and Roasted Fingerling Potatoes on each of 4 serving plates and top with a Gardein breast. Spoon the beurre blanc over the breasts and drizzle a few drops around the edge of each plate. Serve immediately.

Makes 4 servings
Prep time: 30 minutes

old bay tofu cakes
with pan-roasted summer vegetables, horseradish cream, apples, *and* beets

An underlayer of corn, peas, and cherry tomatoes completes this Southern meal.

There are some great rubs and marinades made for meat that work just as well on vegetarian ingredients—so don't shun the meat department entirely. When you think of crab cakes, the flavors that pop into your mind (or your mouth) are celery salt and paprika—Old Bay seasoning is a perfect shortcut. Apples and beets bring sweetness, and horseradish cream balances that.

For the horseradish cream:

¾ cup vegan mayonnaise
¾ cup regular Cashew Cream (page 26)
2½ tablespoons prepared horseradish

Juice of 1 lemon
Sea salt and freshly ground
   black pepper to taste

For the tofu cakes:

Sea salt
2 tablespoons canola oil
½ cup finely diced onion
½ cup finely diced carrots
2 teaspoons minced garlic
1 sheet nori seaweed

2 pounds firm tofu
2½ tablespoons cornstarch
1 tablespoon Old Bay seasoning
¼ cup nutritional yeast flakes
½ teaspoon white pepper
Juice of 1 lime

For the apples and beets:

1 beet, washed
2 tablespoons balsamic vinegar
1 Fuji apple
1 tablespoon extra-virgin olive oil
Sea salt and freshly ground
   black pepper

To cook and serve:

1 cup panko bread crumbs
1½ tablespoons Old Bay seasoning
Sea salt and freshly ground black pepper
1 cup plain unsweetened soy milk
½ cup canola oil, or more if needed
Pan-Roasted Summer Vegetables
   (recipe follows)

"There are some great rubs and marinades made for meat that work just as well on vegetarian ingredients—so don't shun the meat department entirely."

1   *Make the horseradish cream:* Place all the ingredients in a bowl and mix well. Cover and refrigerate until ready to serve.

2   *Make the tofu cakes:* Place a small sauté pan over medium heat. Sprinkle the bottom with a pinch of salt and heat for 1 minute. Add the oil and heat for 30 seconds, being careful not to let it smoke. This will create a nonstick effect. Add the onion and carrots and sauté until soft, 3 to 5 minutes. Add the garlic and sauté for 1 minute longer. Set aside to cool completely.

3   Holding the nori sheet with tongs, toast it by fanning it over a low gas flame or electric burner, being careful not to burn it and turning it so that all of it gets toasted. If you have a spice grinder or a coffee grinder that you use exclusively for spices, break the nori into pieces, place it in the grinder, and pulse until powdered. Alternatively, crumble it as finely as you can with your hands or pulverize it with a mortar and pestle.

4   Place the onion mixture, nori powder, 1 tablespoon salt, and the remaining tofu cake ingredients in a food processor and pulse until well combined but still chunky. Transfer to a bowl, cover, and refrigerate for 30 minutes.

5   *Make the apples and beets:* Place the beet in a small saucepan. Fill with water to cover and add the vinegar. Bring to a boil and cook until you can easily insert a toothpick into the center, about 25 minutes. Drain and peel the beet (a spoon works well). Finely dice the beet and put it in a small bowl. Finely dice the apple and add it to the bowl. Add the oil and salt and pepper to taste; toss to combine. Set aside.

6   *Cook the tofu cakes:* In a shallow dish, stir together the bread crumbs, Old Bay, and 1 teaspoon each of salt and pepper. Pour the soy milk into a separate bowl. Using your hands, form 12 small cakes from the tofu mixture. Dip both sides of each tofu cake in the soy milk, then press into the bread crumbs, coating well. Place the cakes on a baking sheet lined with parchment paper. Refrigerate for 30 minutes, or until firm.

7   Place a sauté pan over medium-high heat. Sprinkle the bottom with a pinch of salt and heat for 1 minute. Add the oil and heat for 2 minutes, being careful not to let it smoke.

8   Working in batches, sauté the tofu cakes (make certain that the oil comes about halfway up the sides of the cakes) until browned on both sides and heated through, 2 to 3 minutes on each side. Remove the cakes to a second baking sheet lined with parchment paper and place in a warm oven until you finish all of the cakes.

9   *Assemble the dish:* Scoop a large spoonful of the Pan-Roasted Summer Vegetables onto the center of each of 6 small serving plates. Place two cakes side by side on top of the vegetables. Top the cakes with a spoonful of the apples and beets and drizzle with the horseradish cream.

Makes 6 servings
Prep time: 1½ hours

✳ pan-roasted **summer vegetables**

Sea salt
2 tablespoons extra-virgin olive oil
1 shallot, minced
2½ cups fresh corn kernels
    (from 3 medium ears)

1 cup fresh or thawed frozen peas
1½ cups cherry tomatoes, halved
3 large basil leaves, cut into
    chiffonade
Freshly ground black pepper

Place a large cast-iron skillet over medium heat. Sprinkle the bottom with a pinch of salt and heat for 1 minute. Add the oil and heat for 30 seconds, being careful not to let it smoke. This will create a nonstick effect.

Add the shallot and sauté for 3 minutes. Add the corn and peas and sauté for 3 minutes. Add the tomatoes and basil and season with salt and pepper to taste. Cook for about 2 minutes, until just heated through. Serve hot.

Makes 5 cups

peppercorn-encrusted
portobello fillets *with*
yellow tomato béarnaise
and mashed potatoes

✳

A meaty mushroom holds up to strong seasoning.

This recipe treats portobellos like pieces of steak. Peppered, seared, and sliced on the bias, they have the heft of a hearty main course and can take on a rich sauce. A classic béarnaise sauce begins with a hollandaise. My friend and great chef Magdiale Wolmark first inspired me to use yellow tomatoes (for their bright, yolky color) to make the béarnaise.

For the portobello fillets:

Sea salt
¼ cup extra-virgin olive oil
2 shallots, chopped
2 garlic cloves, minced

½ cup dry white wine
1½ tablespoons white wine vinegar
4 portobello mushrooms, stemmed, gills removed

For the yellow tomato béarnaise:

4 ripe yellow tomatoes
¼ cup plus 2 tablespoons extra-virgin olive oil
1 teaspoon Dijon mustard
Pinch of white pepper
2 tablespoons white vinegar or white wine vinegar

Sea salt
1 shallot, minced
1 tablespoon minced fresh tarragon
1 cup dry white wine
2 teaspoons arrowroot powder, mixed with ¼ cup cold water (if needed)
3 tablespoons Earth Balance

To cook and serve:

1 teaspoon black peppercorns, crushed in a mortar and pestle or with the back of a spoon
½ teaspoon sea salt
1 teaspoon minced fresh thyme
Mashed Potatoes (recipe follows)

1   *Make the portobello fillets:* Place a large pot over medium heat. Sprinkle the bottom with a pinch of salt and heat for 1 minute. Add the oil and heat for 1 minute, being careful not to let it smoke. This will create a nonstick effect.

2   Add the shallots and garlic and cook for 5 minutes. Add the wine, vinegar, and 1 cup water, bring to a boil, then lower the heat and simmer for 20 minutes.

3   Add the mushrooms and cook for 1 minute. Pour the mushrooms and liquid into a shallow container, cover, and set aside to marinate for 1 hour.

4   *Make the yellow tomato béarnaise:* Preheat the oven to 300°F. Put the tomatoes on a baking sheet and drizzle with 1 tablespoon of the oil, turning to coat well. Roast for 30 minutes, then turn them over and roast for 10 more minutes.

5   Transfer the tomatoes to a blender or food processor; blend until smooth. With the motor running, slowly add the ¼ cup oil and the mustard, white pepper, and vinegar through the hole in the lid, blending until fully emulsified. Pass the sauce through a fine-mesh sieve into a bowl and set aside.

6   Place a large sauté pan over medium heat. Sprinkle the bottom with a pinch of salt and heat for 1 minute. Add the remaining 1 tablespoon oil and heat for 30 seconds, being careful not to let it smoke.

7   Add the shallot and sauté for 2 minutes. Add the tarragon and sauté, stirring frequently to make sure the shallots don't brown, for 2 minutes. Add the wine and cook until reduced by half, about 5 minutes.

8   Add the tomato emulsion and bring to a simmer, then turn off the heat. If the sauce is too thin, before you turn off the heat, whisk in the arrowroot mixture. Remove from the heat and vigorously whisk in the Earth Balance, 1 tablespoon at a time. Adjust the seasonings if necessary. Set the sauce aside, covered to keep warm.

9   *Sear the mushrooms:* Remove the mushrooms from the marinade and press between paper towels or in a cotton dish towel to remove the excess marinade. Sprinkle with the crushed peppercorns, salt, and thyme, pressing the seasoning into both sides of the mushroom pieces. Discard the marinade.

✳ mashed **potatoes**

5 medium white potatoes, peeled and diced	2 tablespoons Earth Balance
⅓ cup regular Cashew Cream (page 26), or more if needed	2 tablespoons minced fresh chives
	Sea salt and freshly ground black pepper

Place the potatoes in a large pot, cover with water, and bring to a boil. Cook, uncovered, for 10 to 15 minutes, until the potatoes are tender. Drain. Place the potatoes in the bowl of a stand mixer fitted with the whisk attachment. (Alternatively, put them in a large bowl and use a handheld mixer.) Add the Cashew Cream, Earth Balance, and chives. Whip on medium-high speed, seasoning with salt and pepper to taste, until smooth and fluffy.

Makes 4 servings

10   Place a large cast-iron skillet over medium-high heat for 1 minute, then add the mushrooms in one layer, working in batches if necessary. Cook until browned and crisp, 2 to 3 minutes on each side.

11   *Assemble the dish:* Slice the mushrooms on the bias into ¼-inch slices, keeping them intact at the base. Fan each mushroom out and lean it against a scoop of Mashed Potatoes. Spoon sauce over the top and drizzle it around the rim of the plate.

Makes 4 servings
Prep time: 1 hour, 45 minutes

free-form ravioli
with tofu ricotta *and* arugula pesto

This is a beautifully rustic version of traditional ravioli, with an added element—fresh herbs rolled in the dough. It's nice to be able to see the flat-leaf parsley in the pasta, and since you don't have to formally roll, cut, and crimp the dumplings, there's a free-form, casual feel to this dish.

For the pasta dough:

4 ounces silken tofu
1 tablespoon extra-virgin olive oil
1 tablespoon red palm oil

½ teaspoon sea salt
2 cups semolina flour, plus
   more for dusting

For the arugula pesto:

¼ cup pine nuts
3 garlic cloves, minced
2 cups coarsely chopped arugula,
   stems included
¼ cup coarsely chopped fresh basil
2 tablespoons nutritional yeast flakes

Sea salt and freshly ground
   black pepper to taste
Pinch of ground cayenne
½ cup extra-virgin olive oil

For the filling:

8 ounces firm tofu, pressed well in a towel
   to remove most of the moisture
1½ teaspoons nutritional yeast flakes
½ teaspoon dried granulated onion
Juice of ½ lemon

¼ cup thick Cashew Cream (page 26)
1½ teaspoons white miso paste
½ teaspoon sea salt
⅛ teaspoon freshly ground
   black pepper

To assemble:

10 sprigs fresh flat-leaf parsley, leaves only

1   *Make the pasta dough:* Place the tofu, olive oil, red palm oil, 2 tablespoons cold water, and the salt in a food processor or blender and blend on high for 1 minute.

2   If using a food processor, gradually add the flour, ½ cup at a time, to the tofu mixture and pulse to combine, adding more water if necessary to make a smooth dough. Once combined, turn the dough out onto a lightly floured surface and knead by hand for 5 to 10 minutes, or transfer the dough to a stand mixer fitted with a dough hook and knead on low speed for 5 minutes.

3   If using a blender, set the tofu mixture aside and mound the flour on a work surface. Make a well in the middle of the flour and pour the tofu mixture into it. Using a fork or your fingers, begin to incorporate the flour into the tofu mixture, starting at the inner rim of the well. Keep pushing flour up from the base of the mound to retain the well shape. When the dough comes together, push aside any loose scraps or excess flour and knead the dough for 5 to 10 minutes, pulling in extra flour or adding a bit more water if needed to form a firm, springy dough. Wrap in plastic wrap and let rest in the refrigerator for 30 minutes.

4   *Make the arugula pesto:* Place all of the pesto ingredients except the oil in a food processor and pulse several times. Continue to blend as you slowly pour in the oil in a thin stream.

5   *Make the filling:* Place all of the filling ingredients in a food processor and pulse until the mixture has the texture of ricotta cheese.

6   *Assemble the ravioli:* Divide the pasta dough into quarters and roll one piece through a pasta machine on the thinnest setting, cutting the sheet in half crosswise if necessary to keep it manageable. Repeat with a second piece of dough. (Save the remaining dough for another use.)

7   Place the two rolled sheets of dough next to each other on a lightly floured surface. Lay parsley leaves randomly over one sheet. Cover with the other sheet of dough, gently press the sheets together, then run the dough through the machine again on the thinnest setting. Place the sheet back on the floured surface and cut it crosswise to make 5-inch squares.

8   Cook the pasta in a large pot of boiling water until it floats, about 3 minutes. Drain.

9   Heat the filling for a few seconds in a microwave oven or in a saucepan over medium heat until warmed through.

10 Working quickly but carefully so that you don't burn your fingers, set the pasta pieces out on a clean, stick-free surface (such as a plastic cutting board). Place 2 tablespoons of the filling in the middle of each piece of pasta, then fold in half to make free-form, imperfect (not totally sealed) ravioli.

11 Divide the ravioli among serving plates and top with a spoonful or two of the arugula pesto. Serve immediately.

Makes 4 servings
Prep time: 1 hour

tempeh creole *over* brown rice

Tempeh's nutty texture is perfect for stews. Because it's so dense, I always braise it to soften it up, even when I plan to pan-fry it later. For this New Orleans–style dish, braising makes the tempeh savory enough to soak up the Creole seasonings. If you braise a little extra tempeh, you can save it in the fridge for a couple of days, then crisp it up in a pan for great sandwiches.

8 tablespoons shoyu soy sauce
4 tablespoons low-salt Creole seasoning
1-inch piece fresh ginger, sliced
⅛ inch thick
2 garlic cloves, sliced
2 (1-inch) pieces kombu seaweed
2 (8-ounce) packages tempeh
½ cup unbleached all-purpose flour
Sea salt
4 tablespoons canola oil, or more if needed
2 cups chopped onions
1 cup chopped bell pepper
1 cup chopped celery

2 cups peeled, seeded, and chopped
fresh tomatoes
1 tablespoon minced garlic
5 bay leaves
¼ teaspoon dried thyme
¼ teaspoon dried oregano
¼ teaspoon dried basil
½ cup dry red wine
Freshly ground black pepper
Ground cayenne
3 tablespoons chopped scallion
2 tablespoons minced fresh parsley
Steamed white or brown rice

1   In a large pot, combine the shoyu, 2 tablespoons of the Creole seasoning, the ginger, sliced garlic, kombu, and 6 cups water and bring to a boil. Cut each slab of tempeh on the bias into ¼-inch slices. Place the tempeh in the boiling broth, reduce the heat, and simmer for 45 minutes. Remove the tempeh with a slotted spoon to a plate and reserve the cooking liquid. In a mixing bowl, stir together the remaining 2 tablespoons Creole seasoning and the flour. Dredge each piece of tempeh in the mixture, coating it well.

2   Place a large sauté pan over medium heat. Sprinkle the bottom with a pinch of salt and heat for 1 minute. Add the oil and heat for 30 seconds, being careful not to let it smoke. This will create a nonstick effect. Add the tempeh, in batches if necessary, and cook until well browned, 2 to 3 minutes on each side. Remove from the pan and set aside. Add the onion, bell pepper, and celery to the pan. Cook, stirring frequently, for about 5 minutes, until the vegetables are just softened. Add the tomatoes and minced garlic. Cook for 3 minutes.

3   Add the reserved tempeh cooking liquid, the bay leaves, thyme, oregano, basil, and wine. Season with salt, black pepper, and cayenne to taste. Gently return the tempeh to the pan, nestling the slices in the liquid. Bring to a simmer and cook, uncovered, for 30 minutes. Remove the bay leaves. Serve in individual bowls over rice, garnished with the scallion and parsley.

Makes 6 to 8 servings
Prep time: 2 hours

my favorite
MUSHROOMS

Vegetarian cooks depend on mushrooms for their dense flavor and meaty texture. But they're also a good source of B vitamins, potassium, and vitamin D. To clean mushrooms, just wipe them off with a damp paper towel. Don't rinse or immerse them, because they can absorb water, and that compromises their texture.

white beech

shiitake

porcini

king oyster (pleurotte)
The stems are edible. If you cut them in 1-inch pieces, they look like scallops. I roast them and serve them with pasta.

chanterelle

black trumpet

enoki Really nice grilled. Leave them in a little bunch and baste them with a mixture of oil, mirin, and tamari.

blue foot

morel Earthy, delicious, and adorable on the plate. They're great crisped in a pan and can stand up to bolder flavors, like wine.

gardein "chicken" scaloppini *with* shiitake sake sauce, braised pea shoots, *and* crispy udon noodle cakes

This is a mash-up of my French and Japanese influences, with a very American meat-and-pasta sensibility. "Scaloppini" refers, of course, to a thin cut of meat, which here is Gardein, a vegan substitute that's a great transitional food for meat-eaters (see page 135). Instead of European wine, this sauce calls for sake, and shiitakes are swapped in for traditional button mushrooms. The udon noodle cakes and pea shoots are another Asian touch, but the overall complexity and lushness of the dish give it a French feel.

For the udon noodle cakes:

4 (7-ounce single-serving) packs precooked udon noodles, still in their packages (see note)
Sea salt
2 tablespoons extra-virgin olive oil
Freshly ground black pepper

For the pea shoots:

Pinch of sea salt
1 tablespoon sesame oil
2 garlic cloves, minced
¼ cup faux chicken stock
2 cups packed pea shoots

ABOUT UDON NOODLES:
Cooked (not dried) udon noodles are available in plastic packages in the refrigerated section of Asian grocery stores. Some are sold in bags of 3 individual servings with an envelope of seasonings, which won't be used in this recipe.

For the chicken:

4 Gardein breasts
Sea salt and freshly ground black pepper
½ cup unbleached all-purpose flour
4 tablespoons extra-virgin olive oil
1 pound shiitake mushrooms, stemmed and cut into ¼-inch slices

1 cup dry sake
½ cup faux chicken stock
½ cup Earth Balance
1 tablespoon minced fresh chives
Microgreens to garnish

1   *Make the udon noodle cakes:* Preheat the oven to 200°F. Remove the plastic from the noodles, keeping the noodles tightly packed. Using a 3-inch round cutter or ring mold, cut one round of noodles from each pack.

2   Place a large sauté pan over high heat. Sprinkle the bottom with a pinch of salt and heat for 1 minute. Add the oil and heat for 30 seconds, being careful not to let it smoke. This will create a nonstick effect.

3   Add the noodle cakes and fry until browned and crisp on both sides, seasoning with salt and pepper as they cook, about 3 minutes per side. Remove to a paper-towel-lined baking sheet and put in the oven to keep warm.

4   *Make the chicken:* Flatten the Gardein breasts with your hand to ½ inch thick, then cut each into 3 pieces. Season with salt and pepper, then dredge in the flour.

5   Wipe out the pan you used for the noodle cakes and add 2 tablespoons of the oil. Heat over medium heat, then add the Gardein pieces and cook until browned, about 3 minutes on each side. Remove to a plate and set aside.

6   Add the remaining 2 tablespoons oil, heat over medium heat, then add the mushrooms and cook for 3 to 4 minutes, stirring often, until softened. Deglaze the pan with the sake and cook until reduced by half, 2 to 3 minutes. Add the stock and cook for 2 more minutes.

7   Remove from the heat and whisk in the Earth Balance 1 tablespoon at a time, whisking constantly so that the sauce doesn't separate. Stir in the chives. Return the Gardein to the pan and toss to coat it with the sauce. Cover to keep warm while you make the pea shoots.

8   *Make the pea shoots:* Place a medium sauté pan over medium heat. Sprinkle the bottom with a pinch of salt and heat for 1 minute. Add the oil and heat for 30 seconds, being careful not to let it smoke.

9   Add the garlic and sauté for 30 seconds. Add the stock and pea shoots and sauté for 3 to 5 minutes, until wilted. Drain the excess liquid.

10 *Assemble the dish:* Place a noodle cake in the center of each plate. Top each cake with a spoonful of pea shoots, then top the pea shoots with 3 pieces of the Gardein. Spoon a little of the sake and mushroom sauce over the Gardein and drizzle it around the plate. Garnish with microgreens and serve immediately.

Makes 4 servings
Prep time: 45 minutes

MEAT-LIKE FOODS, PAST, PRESENT, AND FUTURE: Yves Potvin

FOUNDER OF GARDEIN FROM GARDEN PROTEIN INTERNATIONAL, INC., VANCOUVER, B.C.
PAST OWNER AND FOUNDER OF YVES VEGGIE CUISINE

My friend Yves is a charming guy from Canada who speaks fluent French, English, and Spanish. He's passionate about life and about making it easy for people to eat healthy foods. In fact, Yves created the original veggie hot dog and continues to be an innovator in meat-like foods. Recently, Yves created the first meat-like food that everyday people and chefs could actually cook with. It's called Gardein, a blend of healthy veggies and grains slow-cooked to have the texture and nutrition of premium lean meat. I've used it in the recipes on pages 106, 118, 134, and 154.

TAL: How did your culinary career begin?

YVES: I was trained in French cooking at a school outside of Montreal. After school I traveled to Central America to volunteer at a mission in Guatemala. This was humbling and inspiring work. We would screen children in need of medical attention. Being raised in North America, we often take our health for granted. Traveling to countries less fortunate helped me realize this, and it was a good lesson that I have carried with me. Now I live my life to the fullest. (I like to say I'm an epicurean of life.)

After I returned home, I tried to put the lessons I learned into practice. I worked at a variety of restaurants, though I soon realized something was missing; I wanted to achieve more with my life. That's when I decided I needed to find "my spot." So I got on my bicycle and rode across Canada for inspiration—as the saying goes, "Go West, young man!"

T: You left the "chef hat" behind and biked from Quebec to Vancouver?

Y: Yes. I cycled 3,200 miles and arrived rejuvenated. I was euphoric and believed I could achieve anything! Along the way, I had plenty of time to reflect on my skills and values. I thought to myself, I'm a health-conscious chef, I'm persistent, I'm an entrepreneur, and, most important, I love to help people. It was the 1980s. I saw the growth of dual-income families who were able to afford two cars but had no time to cook. I saw more people jogging, and aerobics was becoming huge, but there was a lack of healthy and convenient foods. I saw the health risks of our high-cholesterol diets all over the news. Putting all this together, I came up with my "aha!" moment: People needed a healthy and convenient food. Soon after this, I learned that 50 million hot dogs were consumed every year in America, so I thought, Why not make a healthy one? That's when I came up with my idea for the original veggie hot dog.

T: A hot dog? And why a veggie one?

Y: Originally I was thinking meat, but meat equals bad cholesterol. Then I met a professor who told me about the benefits of soy protein: cholesterol-free, low in fat, and high in protein.

   At first, I had to make everything by hand: I'd grind the soybeans, add wheat and flavor—very much like making bread. At the time, I worked at an upscale French restaurant at night, and by day the owner let me use the kitchen to refine my recipe. I played around with a variety of ingredients—different veggies and grains. In the end, it took me a year to perfect. I had $5,000 and asked my brother and sister if they would match the amount. Everybody thought I was crazy! When I sold the company in 2001, we were on track for approximately $60 million in annual sales.

T: Then you started another company in 2004. Would you consider yourself to be a serial entrepreneur?

Y: I guess you could say that. When I sold my veggie dog business, I felt my mission was only half done: I'd created a healthier product, but I still felt people were having to compromise in pursuit of healthier meat-like foods. I see Gardein as a big step forward. It has all the health benefits of eating less meat without sacrificing the texture that meat-reducers naturally love. I also believed the category was stuck between the bun— you know, hot dogs, hamburgers, patties, etc. I wanted to offer people more options. That's why I started Garden Protein. I love running the business, but my passion is on the creative side of it, developing new products with a team of chefs. You can do so much with plant-based proteins—different shapes, flavors, and textures. Right now, we've barely scratched the surface.

T: Tell us about Gardein.

Y: First, I should point out that the name Gardein is a combination of "garden" and "protein." It's a meat-like food made from veggies and grains that appeals to meat-lovers and veggie-lovers alike. For health-conscious people it's ideal—it's high in protein, low in fat, cholesterol-free, and contains no animal products.

T: Some people worry that turning veggies into meat-like foods requires a lot of processing.

Y: It doesn't. The secret is in how we blend the ingredients together. The Gardein is then slow-cooked in special ovens to give it its meaty mouth-feel.

T: What do you hope the future holds for Gardein?

Y: In the next 30 years, the Earth's population is forecasted to reach 10 billion people, and demand for protein is expected to double. How are we going to feed all of these people and protect our environment? I believe plant-based protein is a critical part of the solution. Everyone should have access to choices that can make the world a better place now and for future generations.

Today, Gardein is in about 4,000 stores across North America and growing. Our foods continue to evolve, and we continue to innovate. (We've recently added ancient grains—quinoa, amaranth, millet and kamut.) My vision is to see Gardein on menus nationwide simply as the healthy protein option—as in, you can have the salad with chicken, fish, or Gardein. When that happens, I'll feel much closer to achieving what I was inspired to do from my experiences in Guatemala and on that long road across North America.

But it's not only my goal anymore. Everyone at Garden Protein is passionate about Gardein being part of the solution. We believe eating more plant-based foods builds good health and is good for our planet, too. It's part of the reason we like to say that "goodness grows."

paella *with* "sausage," nori-dusted oyster mushrooms, *and* wine-braised artichoke hearts

* Here, oyster mushrooms stand in for seafood.

The sausage I use in this recipe is made by a great company called Field Roast. It's made from wheat protein, kind of like seitan, which is a protein developed 2,000 years ago by Buddhist monks. I usually opt for Field Roast's Italian sausage, but if you want some extra spice, go for the chipotle. It's fine to use canned artichoke hearts—get the ones that are packed in water, not oil, and rinse and dry them well. You can add a light taste of the ocean with nori dust.

For the rice:

Sea salt
4 tablespoons extra-virgin olive oil
1 red onion, diced
3 garlic cloves, minced
2 tablespoons minced fresh parsley
2 tomatoes, peeled and finely chopped
1 red bell pepper, diced

1 green bell pepper, diced
1½ cups Bomba paella rice or any
    medium-grain rice
4 cups faux chicken or vegetable stock
Pinch of saffron threads
½ teaspoon freshly ground
    black pepper

For the toppings:

Sea salt
3 tablespoons extra-virgin olive oil
3 Field Roast Italian-Style seitan
    sausages, cut on an extreme bias
    into ¼-inch-thick slices
2 pounds oyster mushrooms
1 sheet nori seaweed, toasted and ground
    to a fine powder (see page 140, step 3)

Freshly ground black pepper
1 (14-ounce) can artichoke hearts,
    drained and cut in half
½ cup dry white wine
Juice of 1 lemon
½ cup frozen peas, thawed
Lemon wedges

1   *Make the rice:* Place a 15-inch paella pan or a large sauté pan over medium heat. Sprinkle the bottom with a pinch of salt and heat for 1 minute. Add 2 tablespoons of the oil and heat for 30 seconds, being careful not to let it smoke. This will create a nonstick effect.

2   Add the onion, garlic, and parsley and cook for 5 minutes, stirring frequently. Add the tomatoes and a splash of water and cook until the liquid has evaporated and the mixture is thick like jam, about 10 minutes. Transfer this sofrito to a bowl. Wipe the pan clean.

3   Return the pan to medium heat, add the remaining 2 tablespoons oil, then add the red and green peppers and sauté for 5 minutes.

4   Return the sofrito to the pan, along with the rice. Stir and cook for 2 minutes. Add the stock, saffron, 1 teaspoon salt, and the pepper. Stir well, then bring to a boil and cook, uncovered, for 10 minutes without stirring. Lower the heat to a simmer and continue cooking, uncovered and without stirring, for 15 minutes.

5   *Make the toppings:* Place a medium sauté pan over medium heat. Sprinkle the bottom with a pinch of salt and heat for 1 minute. Add 1 tablespoon of the oil and heat for 30 seconds, being careful not to let it smoke. Add the sausages and cook until crisp on both sides, about 5 minutes total. Remove to a plate. Wipe the pan clean.

6   Return the pan to medium heat, add 1 tablespoon of the oil, then add the mushrooms and sauté, seasoning with the nori dust and salt and pepper to taste, until they have released their liquid and are nicely browned and crisp on the outside, 5 to 7 minutes. Remove from the pan and set aside. Wipe the pan clean.

7   Return the pan to medium heat, add the remaining 1 tablespoon oil, then add the artichoke hearts and sauté, seasoning with salt and pepper, until lightly browned, about 3 minutes. Add the wine and cook until it has almost completely evaporated, about 10 minutes. Remove the pan from heat and stir in the lemon juice.

8   Increase the heat under the rice mixture to high and cook for 2 to 3 minutes, or until you smell the rice toasting (but not burning) on the bottom. Remove from the heat.

9   Sprinkle the peas over the top, cover the pan with aluminum foil, and let rest for 5 minutes. Remove the foil and scatter the sausage, mushrooms, and artichokes over the top. Serve with lemon wedges.

Makes 6 to 8 servings
Prep time: 1 hour, 10 minutes

What exactly is SEITAN?

✳ Seitan is just gluten—the protein that's left after the starch is removed from wheat. Thanks to its chewy, sometimes stringy texture, it's evocative of meat, and you'll find lots of seitan-based meat replacements in the fridge at places like Whole Foods. You can make your own seitan, but it's pretty complicated; I tend to use packaged options. Plain seitan takes on the flavor of whatever you cook it in. It's really high in protein—with about 30 grams per serving it's near the top of the list of plant-based sources. Packaged seitan products are great for adding a hefty, meaty bite to a vegan dish, and a nice transitional option for meat-eaters venturing into new territory.

artichoke ricotta tortellini *with* saffron cream sauce

The homemade pasta recipe here is adapted from one I learned back in school at the Natural Gourmet Institute. Chef Dave Anderson, of Madeleine Bistro in L.A., turned me on to the idea of using red palm oil for a yolky color. It's a great trick. When you make pasta from scratch, it's a good idea to set out all of your ingredients in advance to make the process smoother. This is a rich, satisfying dish. It's as much fun to make with friends as it is to eat.

4 ounces silken tofu
1 tablespoon extra-virgin olive oil
1 tablespoon red palm oil
½ teaspoon sea salt
2 cups semolina flour, plus more for dusting

For the filling:

Sea salt
2 tablespoons olive oil
1 (14-ounce) can artichoke hearts,
    drained and roughly chopped
2 garlic cloves

¼ cup dry white wine
2 cups regular Cashew Cream
    (page 26)
¼ cup nutritional yeast flakes
Freshly ground black pepper

For the saffron cream sauce:

Sea salt
1 tablespoon extra-virgin olive oil
1 small shallot, minced
½ cup dry white wine
1 cup regular Cashew Cream (page 26)

1 tablespoon nutritional yeast flakes
Pinch of saffron threads
Freshly ground black pepper
4 tablespoons Earth Balance

To serve:

6 cups fresh baby arugula
4 plum tomatoes, cut into thin
    wedges, seeds and inner
    flesh removed

1   *Make the pasta dough:* Place the tofu, olive oil, red palm oil, 2 tablespoons cold water, and the salt in a food processor or blender and blend on high for 1 minute.

2   If using a food processor, gradually add the flour, ½ cup at a time, to the tofu mixture and pulse to combine, adding more water if necessary to make a smooth dough. Once combined, turn the dough out onto a lightly floured surface and knead by hand for 5 to 10 minutes, or transfer to a stand mixer fitted with a dough hook and knead on low speed for 5 minutes.

3   If using a blender, set the tofu mixture aside and mound the flour on a work surface. Make a well in the middle of the flour and pour the tofu mixture into the well. Using a fork or your fingers, begin to incorporate the flour into the tofu mixture, starting at the inner rim of the well. Keep pushing the flour up from the base of the mound to retain the well shape. When the dough comes together, push aside any loose scraps or excess flour and knead the dough for 5 to 10 minutes, pulling in extra flour or adding a bit more water if needed to form a firm, springy dough. Wrap in plastic wrap and let it rest in the refrigerator for 30 minutes.

4   *Make the filling:* Place a sauté pan over medium heat. Sprinkle the bottom with a pinch of salt and heat for 1 minute. Add the oil and heat for 30 seconds, being careful not to let it smoke. This will create a nonstick effect.

5   Add the artichoke hearts and garlic and sauté for 2 to 3 minutes, until the garlic is softened but not browned. Deglaze the pan with the wine and cook until almost all the wine has evaporated. Add the Cashew Cream and stir well. Add the nutritional yeast, season with salt and pepper to taste, and stir well. Cool for about 10 minutes, until thickened. Pulse the artichoke mixture in a food processor until a texture similar to that of ricotta is achieved.

6   *Assemble the pasta:* Pull off a small piece of pasta dough. Rewrap the remaining dough in the plastic wrap and return it to the refrigerator. Set a pasta machine on its widest setting and press the dough through the machine 2 or 3 times. Pull the dough as it emerges from the machine to form a more uniform rectangle, and dust with flour as needed. Reduce the machine setting and run the dough through 2 or 3 more times. Continue tightening the setting and running the dough through until the machine is on the narrowest setting.

7 Lay the dough on a work surface. Using a 3-inch ring mold or round cutter, cut circles out of the dough. Place 1 teaspoon of the artichoke filling in the center of each circle. Fold the dough over the filling, pressing to seal the edges, and bend into a circular tortellini shape. Place on a lightly floured baking sheet and cover with plastic wrap. Repeat with the remaining dough and filling. (You will have extra dough; roll it out and cut it into fettuccine or pappardelle, if you'd like, or refrigerate it for several days.)

8 *Make the saffron cream sauce:* Place a medium sauté pan over medium heat. Sprinkle the bottom with a pinch of salt and heat for 1 minute. Add the oil and heat for 30 seconds, being careful not to let it smoke.

"This dish is as much fun to make with friends as it is to eat."

9 Add the shallot and sauté for 2 to 3 minutes, being careful not to let it brown. Add the wine and cook until it has reduced by half, about 5 minutes. Whisk in the Cashew Cream, nutritional yeast, and saffron and cook for 5 minutes, stirring constantly. Season with salt and pepper to taste. Remove from the heat. Whisk in the Earth Balance 1 tablespoon at a time.

10 *Cook and serve the tortellini:* Fill a large pot with water and 1 teaspoon salt and bring to a boil over high heat. Add the tortellini, return the water to a boil, and cook for 3 minutes. Using a slotted spoon, remove the tortellini to the pan with the saffron cream sauce and pile the arugula and tomato wedges on top. Gently toss over low heat to heat through and serve immediately.

Makes 6 servings
Prep time: 2 hours

Chef Profile

RESTAURANT:
Madeleine Bistro in
Los Angeles

SPECIALTY:
Adventurous, elegant
vegan cuisine

PERSONAL ORIENTATION:
Vegan

GUEST CHEF:
Dave Anderson

✳ *"After my family, veganism is my life. Human beings have evolved beyond the need to consume animals as a means to survive. Therefore, eating meat is a luxury, and one that seems unnecessarily cruel and twisted. The next logical step seems to be for us to evolve beyond our instinctual craving for animal flesh. In a spiritual way, I feel that I've been given the gift to create food that will help people overcome their need for this antiquated way of eating."*

Dave Anderson is a mentor of mine and definitely one of my biggest influences. He's probably the most innovative vegan chef out there. I worked for Dave at his restaurant, Madeleine Bistro in L.A., a fantastic, progressive place where you can get dishes found nowhere else. One of the things Dave is best known for is making everything from scratch. When I worked at his restaurant we would make our own vegan egg yolks, egg whites, and butter, and then we'd use these throughout the cooking. His homemade vegan Chardonnay cheese (which I remember having as far back as 2004) is amazing, as are his desserts. Dave makes a better chocolate soufflé without eggs than anyone on earth.

Chef Dave Anderson

MENU:

APPETIZER

Asian Tacos with Kinpira and Spinach-Sesame Salad

SALAD

Beet Mosaic with Gold Beet Vinaigrette, Balsamic Glaze, and Cucumber Salad

ENTRÉE

Grilled Shiitake Mushrooms with Polenta, Roasted Japanese Eggplant, and Smoked-Paprika Crème

Asian Tacos with Kinpira and Spinach-Sesame Salad

FOR THE KINPIRA:
½ tablespoon canola oil
1 cup peeled and julienned burdock
½ cup peeled and julienned carrot
1½ tablespoons mirin
½ tablespoon evaporated cane juice
½ tablespoon soy sauce
½ tablespoon tamari
½ tablespoon sesame seeds

FOR THE SESAME DRESSING:
2 tablespoons brown rice vinegar
2 tablespoons evaporated cane juice
½ teaspoon Dijon mustard
5 tablespoons canola oil
1 tablespoon sesame oil
½ tablespoon sesame seeds
Sea salt and freshly ground black pepper

FOR THE TACO SHELLS:
Canola oil for deep-frying
16 (3½-inch) round wonton skins

FOR THE FILLING:
½ tablespoon canola oil
½ tablespoon minced ginger
½ tablespoon minced garlic
4 cups finely diced seitan
4 cups shredded napa cabbage
2 tablespoons soy sauce
2 tablespoons mirin
2 tablespoons light agave nectar

TO SERVE:
1 bunch spinach, washed, stemmed, and
    blanched in boiling water for 20 seconds
Sea salt
1 cup shredded napa cabbage
Sesame seeds

Make the kinpira:
In a wok or large skillet, heat the oil over medium-high heat. Add the burdock and stir-fry for 2 minutes. Add the carrot and stir-fry for 2 minutes. Stir in the mirin, cane juice, soy sauce, and 1½ tablespoons water and cook, stirring often, until most of the liquid is absorbed.

   Remove from the heat and stir in the tamari and sesame seeds. Transfer to a platter and chill in the refrigerator for at least 1 hour.

Make the sesame dressing:
In a medium bowl, whisk together the vinegar, cane juice, and mustard. Slowly pour in the oils, whisking constantly, then stir in the sesame seeds. Season to taste with salt and pepper. Transfer to a small container and chill in the refrigerator until ready to use.

Make the taco shells:
Pour 4 inches of oil into a large saucepan. Place over high heat and heat to 350°F. Form a taco shell by holding a wonton with a pair of tongs and folding it over the back of the

tongs with a spoon, creating a U-shape. Submerge in the hot oil and fry until crisp and golden brown, about 1 minute. Remove the taco shell to paper towels to drain. Repeat with the remaining wonton.

Make the filling:
In a wok or large skillet, heat the oil over medium-high heat. Add the ginger and garlic and stir-fry for 1 minute. Add the seitan and stir-fry for about 4 minutes. Stir in the cabbage, soy sauce, mirin, and agave nectar. Stir-fry until the cabbage wilts, about 3 minutes more. Keep warm until ready to serve.

Assemble the tacos:
In a large bowl, toss the spinach with some of the sesame dressing and salt to taste. Place a small bed of shredded cabbage on each of 4 serving plates and lightly drizzle with sesame dressing. Place a small mound of the spinach salad to the left of the cabbage and a small mound of kinpira to the right. Fill each taco shell with 1 tablespoon of filling and 1 teaspoon of cabbage. Place 4 tacos on the bed of cabbage on each plate, wedged between the spinach salad and kinpira. Sprinkle with sesame seeds and serve immediately.

Makes 4 servings
Prep time: 45 minutes, plus 1 hour kinpira chilling

Beet Mosaic with Gold Beet Vinaigrette, Balsamic Glaze, and Cucumber Salad

FOR THE BEET MOSAIC:
2 pounds mixed beets (red, gold, and
   candy-striped or chioggia)
Sea salt
1½ cups filtered water
2 tablespoons agar-agar flakes
Freshly ground black pepper

FOR THE GOLD BEET VINAIGRETTE:
½ cup gold beet scraps (from above)
¼ cup Champagne vinegar
1 tablespoon minced shallot
1 tablespoon light agave nectar
¾ cup extra-virgin olive oil
Sea salt and freshly ground black pepper

FOR THE BALSAMIC GLAZE:
½ cup balsamic vinegar

FOR THE CUCUMBER SALAD:
½ cup finely diced cucumber
2 tablespoons seeded and finely
   diced tomato
2 teaspoons minced fresh chives
2 teaspoons extra-virgin olive oil
Sea salt and freshly ground black pepper

TO SERVE:
2 cups spring greens mix
Sea salt

Make the beet mosaic:
Place the red beets in a large saucepan and cover with salted water. Bring to a boil, then reduce the heat to a simmer and cook until the beets are fork tender. Remove and let cool to room temperature. Peel the beets, then square them off and cut into small, even strips. Repeat with the gold and candy-striped beets (these two can be cooked together). Reserve the trimmings from the gold beets for the vinaigrette.

   Oil the inside of a 5¾ by 3¼-inch loaf pan and line it with plastic wrap. Combine the filtered water and the agar-agar in a small saucepan and bring to a boil over high heat. Reduce to a simmer and cook until the agar-agar is completely melted, 5 to 10 minutes.

   With a pastry brush, brush the bottom of the loaf pan with the agar-agar mixture. Dip a red beet strip in the agar-agar mixture and place it in the corner of the pan. Dip another strip and place it behind the first. It will take a few strips to make a row, and you may need to cut strips to fit. Repeat with strips of gold beet, making a row next to the red-beet one. Repeat with strips of candy-striped beet, making a row next to the gold-beet one. Continue alternating colors until you have made a complete layer, season with salt and pepper, and brush agar-agar over the layer so that any cracks are filled in. Continue building layers of alternating colors until the loaf pan is full. Wrap tightly in plastic wrap. Place a 3- to 4-pound weight on top of the pan and chill for at least 8 hours.

"The Beet Mosaic always reminds me of Tal. One year, I was foolish enough to put it on the Valentine's Day chef's tasting menu. Great dish, right? The problem is we had 100 people booked for a seven-course meal, and this was only one of the courses—and rather labor-intensive. I bellyached to Tal the night before, and he offered to come down and help out. We ended up in the kitchen long past midnight, cutting, dipping, and arranging beets. Somehow we got it done, and we had a great time, too."

Remove the mosaic from the pan and plastic wrap and carefully cut into 10 even slices. Place the slices on a cookie sheet lined with parchment paper. Cover with plastic wrap and chill in the refrigerator until ready to serve.

Make the balsamic glaze:
Place the vinegar in a small saucepan. Bring to a boil, then reduce the heat to a simmer and cook until reduced to 1 tablespoon, about 10 minutes. Pour into a container and chill until ready to serve.

Make the gold beet vinaigrette:
Place the gold beet scraps, vinegar, shallot, and agave nectar in a blender or food processor. Blend until pureed. Slowly drizzle in the oil, blending until emulsified. Season to taste with salt and pepper. Pour into a container and chill until ready to serve.

Make the cucumber salad:
In a small bowl, toss the cucumber, tomato, chives, oil, and salt and pepper to taste until well combined. Set aside.

Assemble the salad:
Place a slice of the beet mosaic in the center of each serving plate. Toss the spring greens in a mixing bowl with a pinch of salt and add some vinaigrette to taste. Place a small mound of green salad at 12 o'clock on each plate. Place two small mounds of cucumber salad at 4 o'clock and 8 o'clock. Drizzle the outer edge of the plate with vinaigrette and balsamic glaze. Serve immediately.

Makes 4 to 6 servings
Prep time: 1 hour, 30 minutes, plus chilling

Grilled Shiitake Mushrooms with Polenta, Roasted Japanese Eggplant, and Smoked-Paprika Crème

FOR THE MUSHROOMS:
12 (3-inch-diameter) shiitake mushroom caps
2 cups extra-virgin olive oil
Sea salt and freshly ground black pepper

FOR THE POLENTA:
2 cups unsweetened plain soy milk
1 teaspoon minced garlic
2½ tablespoons extra-virgin olive oil
Sea salt and freshly ground black pepper
1 cup polenta

FOR THE SMOKED-PAPRIKA CRÈME:
¾ cup whole raw cashews, soaked overnight
    in water to cover, then drained
2 tablespoons plus 1 teaspoon canola oil
1 teaspoon minced shallot
1 teaspoon minced garlic
4 teaspoons smoked paprika
Sea salt and freshly ground black pepper

FOR THE MUSHROOM PUREE:
1 tablespoon extra-virgin olive oil
2 cups diced shiitake mushroom caps
¼ cup diced onion
1 teaspoon minced garlic
Sea salt and freshly ground black pepper

FOR THE ROASTED EGGPLANT:
3 Japanese eggplants, peeled and diced
1 tablespoon extra-virgin olive oil
Sea salt and freshly ground black pepper

TO SERVE:
1 cup haricots verts, stemmed and
    cut in half crosswise
1 cup spinach, stemmed
Microgreens for garnish

Start the mushrooms:
Preheat the oven to 225°F. Place the mushrooms in a single layer in a 9-inch square baking dish. Pour the oil over the mushrooms and cover the dish with aluminum foil. Bake for 2 hours. Remove from the oil and season with salt and pepper to taste (the oil can be saved and used as a mushroom-infused oil). Refrigerate until ready to use.

Start the polenta:
Place the soy milk, 2 quarts water, garlic, oil, and salt and pepper to taste in a large saucepan and bring to a boil over high heat. Reduce to a simmer and slowly pour in the polenta, whisking constantly. Simmer, stirring often, until the polenta is thick but still spreadable, 4 to 5 minutes. Brush a 6-inch square baking dish with oil and pour in the polenta, smoothing the top. Chill in the refrigerator for at least 2 hours.

Make the smoked-paprika crème:
Place the cashews, 1 cup water, and 2 tablespoons of the oil in a blender or food

processor and blend until pureed. In a large saucepan, heat the remaining 1 teaspoon oil over medium-high heat. Add the shallot and sauté until translucent, about 2 minutes. Add the garlic and sauté for 1 minute. Add the cashew puree, bring to a boil, then reduce the heat to a simmer and cook until slightly reduced and thickened.

Transfer to a blender or food processor, add the paprika, and blend until smooth. Pour through a fine-mesh sieve into a bowl and season to taste with salt and pepper. Set aside at room temperature until ready to use.

Make the mushroom puree:
In a large saucepan or wok, heat the oil over medium heat. Add the mushrooms and sauté until softened but not browned, about 5 minutes. Stir in the onion and garlic and sauté until the mushrooms are golden brown.

Place the mushroom mixture and ½ cup water in a blender or food processor and blend until pureed. Season to taste with salt and pepper. Keep warm until ready to use.

Make the roasted eggplant:
Preheat the oven to 350°F. In a large bowl, toss the eggplant with the oil to coat and season to taste with salt and pepper. Transfer to a baking sheet and roast until soft, about 15 minutes. Return to the bowl and set aside.

Finish the mushrooms:
Preheat a charcoal grill to high, or heat a cast-iron grill pan over medium-high heat. Grill the mushrooms until marked on both sides. Keep warm until ready to use.

Finish the polenta:
Cut the polenta into narrow rectangles and season with salt and pepper. In a large skillet, heat the remaining 1 tablespoon oil over medium heat. Add 4 strips of polenta, top side down, and cook until golden brown, about 5 minutes. Turn and cook the other side until golden brown. Keep warm until ready to use.

Assemble the dish:
Bring a medium saucepan of water to a boil and blanch the haricots verts until bright green and cooked through, about 5 minutes. Remove with a slotted spoon to the bowl with the eggplant. Blanch the spinach for 20 seconds, drain, and add the spinach to the bowl with the eggplant. Toss to combine.

Smear 2 tablespoons of the mushroom puree in the center of each of 4 serving plates. Place a rectangle of polenta on top of the puree. Arrange the mixed vegetables on top of the polenta, and put 3 grilled mushrooms on top of the vegetables. Drizzle 1 tablespoon smoked paprika crème around the polenta. Garnish with microgreens and serve immediately.

Makes 4 servings
Prep time: 1 hour, 15 minutes, plus 2 hours polenta chilling

agave-lime grilled tofu *with* asian slaw *and* mashed sweet potatoes

This is an easy recipe that makes a gorgeous, colorful plate—and the leftovers are great for sandwiches. Agave is similar to honey, but it has a lighter taste. The marinade here is sweet and savory, and when you reduce it in the pan after the tofu is cooked, it turns into a wonderfully sticky glaze.

*

Agave and shoyu combine for a sweet and savory glaze.

For the tofu:

1 pound extra-firm tofu, cut into
  8 (¼-inch-thick) slabs
¼ cup light agave nectar
½ cup shoyu soy sauce
3 garlic cloves, smashed
2 sprigs fresh thyme

1 teaspoon freshly ground
  black pepper
Juice of 2 limes
1½ tablespoons lightly
  packed brown sugar

For the slaw:

3 tablespoons rice vinegar
1 teaspoon light agave nectar
½ teaspoon sea salt, or more to taste
2 tablespoons freshly squeezed lime juice
1 teaspoon soy sauce
¼ cup safflower oil

1 large carrot, peeled and julienned
½ daikon radish, peeled and julienned
½ head napa cabbage, shredded
1 scallion, julienned
½ teaspoon mixed black and white
  sesame seeds

For the sweet potatoes:

2 large sweet potatoes, peeled and diced
½ cup thick Cashew Cream (page 26)
2 tablespoons Earth Balance
1 canned chipotle pepper, seeded and minced
Sea salt and freshly ground black pepper

1   *Make the tofu:* Place the tofu in a single layer in a shallow nonreactive dish. In a small bowl, whisk together the remaining tofu ingredients. Pour over the tofu and marinate in the refrigerator for 2 hours.

2   Preheat the oven to 300°F. Lightly oil a baking sheet. Using a slotted spoon, remove the tofu from the marinade (reserve the marinade) and arrange it in a single layer on the baking sheet. Bake for 15 minutes.

3   Meanwhile, pour the marinade into a small saucepan. Cook over medium-high heat until reduced to a syrupy glaze, about 8 minutes.

4   Heat an outdoor grill or preheat a grill pan over medium-high heat. Transfer the tofu slabs from the baking sheet to the grill and grill for 3 to 4 minutes, or until grill-marked. Turn the tofu over and generously brush with the glaze; cook for 3 to 4 minutes, or until grill-marked. Remove the tofu to the baking sheet, turning it over so the glazed side is down, then glaze the top side.

"Asian slaw lightens things up—a fresh, crunchy element that cuts the sweetness of the tofu and enhances the creamy mashed potatoes."

5   *Make the slaw:* In a large bowl, whisk together the vinegar, agave nectar, salt, lime juice, and soy sauce. Continue whisking vigorously in one direction as you slowly pour in the oil in a thin stream until emulsified. Add the remaining slaw ingredients to the bowl and toss to coat.

6   *Make the sweet potatoes:* Cook the sweet potatoes in a pot of boiling water for 20 minutes, or until tender. Drain. Put the sweet potatoes, Cashew Cream, Earth Balance, and chipotle pepper in the bowl of a stand mixer fitted with the whisk attachment. Alternatively, put the ingredients in a large bowl and use a handheld mixer. Whip on medium-high speed until smooth and fluffy. Season with salt and pepper to taste.

7   *Assemble the dish:* Place one quarter of the sweet potatoes in a scoop in the middle of a serving plate. Top with one quarter of the slaw. Place 2 tofu slices on top of the slaw or angled against the sweet potatoes and slaw. Repeat with the remaining ingredients.

Makes 4 servings
Prep time: 1 hour, plus 2 hours marinating

Tips on TOFU:

✳ When you're using firm or extra-firm tofu in a recipe, you always want to get the water out first: After you rinse the tofu, just wrap it in a dish towel, put something heavy on top, and leave it for about 20 minutes. You'll get a denser product that will absorb the flavor of your sauce better. Of course, as with almost everything, the tastiest tofu is homemade, and the process is pretty easy. It's a lot like making mozzarella. You boil soy milk, add a coagulant (usually some kind of salt), then strain the mixture through cheesecloth to catch the curds. The curds go into a mold, which has holes for drainage, with a weight on top to push out the water. That's all there is to it. If you have a soy-milk maker, you can even go back a step and start right from the beans. Whether you go with store-bought tofu or you make your own, if you ever want a chewier texture (for, say, braising recipes), freeze and thaw your tofu before you prepare it—this gives it a more fibrous consistency.

THE RADICAL RESTAURATEURS:

Joy Pierson and Bart Potenza

OWNERS, CANDLE CAFE AND CANDLE 79, NEW YORK, NY

Joy and Bart created one of the first truly elegant fine-dining vegan places with their restaurant Candle 79, which opened in 2003 on New York's Upper East Side. Their Candle Cafe, just a few blocks away, has been around since 1994.

TAL: What was it like opening one of the first fine-dining vegan restaurants in the world?

BART: I don't think either of us stopped to think whether it was a good idea business-wise. We loved the mission, and it felt right.

JOY: I guess it's always difficult to start, and you always have trepidation. We wanted to spread the message that delicious, elegant food can also help heal the planet. We were extremely committed to making a difference.

T: How did customers react?

B: Fortunately, we have a very supportive customer base. They were a bit wary at first, but once they knew what we were about they were hooked, and they started to tell all their friends.

J: It was a slow build. Pure, positive energy helped us create a loyal following of clientele who are dedicated to the mission of health and well-being. For us it's always been about the mission. We really care about what we feed people. Preparing nonviolent food is our way of contributing to world peace. When you follow your passion, all paths open before you.

T: You have a great money story.

B: We do. In 1993, on Friday the 13th, I played Joy's birthday along with mine in the New York State Lottery, and we won $53,000.

J: That was the seed money for Candle Cafe, and we've been growing ever since. But it's really just one example of the many miracles we've been blessed to receive.

T: What came before that?

J: Bart had a tiny little vegetarian juice bar in the neighborhood—500 square feet. I was a nutritionist, and I would come to offer health counseling. Bart made me a sandwich that changed my life. With my own transition to a plant-based diet, I immediately saw the benefits to my physical and emotional well-being. I was inspired by how great I felt!

B: I had an art and marketing background. Destiny led me to the vegan restaurant industry.

T: And you're working on introducing kids to vegan meals?

J: Yes, twice a week we feed a plant-based entree to schoolchildren in Harlem. We also offer children and their families educational programs and dinner once a month.

B: The kids love our food. Our chefs make eating fun and healthy for them, and in return we get to be involved in the community. Outreach has always been important to us. We want to show that veganism can work for everybody.

T: Your places reflect that. They're both very welcoming.

J: Yes, we are a community! Our staff and customers at both restaurants combine to create a close-knit and loving family.

B: Once people enter our doors, their lives are never the same. Patrons new to our cuisine are constantly impressed by the freshness and flavors.

T: Who are your regulars these days?

J: I'd say the majority are not vegetarians. We still have people who are resistant, but I think once they taste the food, they love it. I've seen people who were dragged into the restaurant by a friend but who leave saying, "That was the best meal I've ever had."

B: They're conscientious people choosing to vote with their forks. I've been in this field for 30 years, and I've never seen anything like it, how strongly people want what we serve.

whole wheat penne *with* san marzano tomatoes

This is a quick, easy recipe that's healthful and very bold in flavor. I like both white and whole wheat pasta, but there's a nice depth to whole wheat that adds richness here. The sauce is tangy, thanks to the olives, wine, and fennel. You don't have to be precise about the ingredients. Swap out anything you don't like (or don't have on hand) for whatever works for you—for instance, chard for kale or olives for capers.

Sea salt
3 tablespoons extra-virgin olive oil
2 onions, quartered and sliced
2 fennel bulbs, halved and sliced
1 (28-ounce) can peeled Italian San Marzano tomatoes, drained
4 garlic cloves, minced
½ cup vegetable stock
½ cup white wine
4 cups roughly chopped Swiss chard

Freshly ground black pepper
Juice of 1 lemon
¾ cup Manzanilla (green) olives, roughly chopped
1 tablespoon minced fresh tarragon
1 tablespoon minced fresh thyme
1 tablespoon minced fresh parsley
8 ounces whole wheat penne, cooked al dente according to package directions

1   Place a large sauté pan over medium-high heat. Sprinkle the bottom with a pinch of salt and heat for 1 minute. Add the oil and heat for 30 more seconds, being careful not to let it smoke. This will create a nonstick effect.

2   Add the onions and fennel and cook for 3 to 4 minutes, stirring occasionally. Add the tomatoes, crushing each with your hand, along with the garlic, stock, wine, and chard. Season with salt and pepper to taste. Reduce the heat to medium and cook for 5 minutes.

3   Add the lemon juice and olives and simmer for 3 to 5 minutes, until the olives are tender. Fold in the tarragon, thyme, and parsley, along with the hot pasta. Serve immediately.

Makes 4 servings
Prep time: 30 minutes

asparagus *and* meyer lemon risotto

Meyer lemons are a lot milder and sweeter than regular lemons, so you can use them a little more freely. This is a real spring dish to me, great for the changing weather. It's refreshing, because of the citrus, but still comforting and filling on a chilly night. Cashew cream and nutritional yeast give the risotto extra richness, but it's also creamy and delicious without them, if you prefer.

Sea salt

1 pound asparagus, bottoms trimmed, cut on the bias into 1-inch pieces

Freshly ground black pepper

3 tablespoons extra-virgin olive oil

3 shallots, chopped

2 garlic cloves, chopped

2 cups Arborio rice

1 cup plus a splash of dry white wine

6 cups vegetable stock

Grated zest of 3 Meyer lemons

¼ cup thick Cashew Cream (page 26; optional)

1 tablespoon nutritional yeast flakes (optional)

Juice of 2 Meyer lemons

½ cup pine nuts, toasted

1   Fill a small pot with water. Add 1 teaspoon salt and bring to a boil. Blanch the asparagus in the boiling water for 1 minute, then chill in an ice bath, drain, and sprinkle with a pinch each of salt and pepper. Set aside.

2   Place a large sauté pan with steep sides over medium heat. Sprinkle the bottom with a pinch of salt and heat for 1 minute. Add the oil and heat for 30 seconds, being careful not to let it smoke. This will create a nonstick effect.

3   Add the shallots and sauté for 3 minutes. Add the garlic and sauté for 1 minute. Add a pinch of salt and the rice and sauté for 2 minutes, stirring frequently.

4   Add 1 cup wine and cook, stirring constantly, until it has been completely absorbed and evaporated. Add the stock, 1 cup at a time, cooking and stirring after each addition until all the liquid is absorbed; it should take about 30 minutes to add all the stock. As you cook the rice, season periodically with salt and pepper, tasting after each addition.

5   Fold in the lemon zest, Cashew Cream and nutritional yeast (if using), the asparagus, and a splash of wine and continue cooking for 2 to 3 minutes, until the asparagus is heated through and the risotto is thick and creamy.

6   Remove from the heat and gently stir in the lemon juice. Adjust the seasoning as necessary. Serve immediately with a few toasted pine nuts sprinkled on top.

Makes 6 servings
Prep time: 45 minutes

IF YOU DON'T HAVE MEYER LEMONS:
If you don't have slightly sweet and floral Meyer lemons, use the zest of 2 regular lemons and 1 clementine orange, and the juice of 1 lemon and 1 clementine.

my favorite
SEA VEGETABLES

dulse You can crisp it on the stove or in the oven to add a nice texture to salads and sandwiches. It's also sold smoked, which has a bacony flavor.

There's a huge variety of options in this nutrient-dense category, and once you become comfortable with them, it's hard to imagine cooking without them. Always rinse sea vegetables before you use them, so that they're not too salty.

kombu Not really edible, because it's very tough, but it's great for making soups and stocks if you rinse it well.

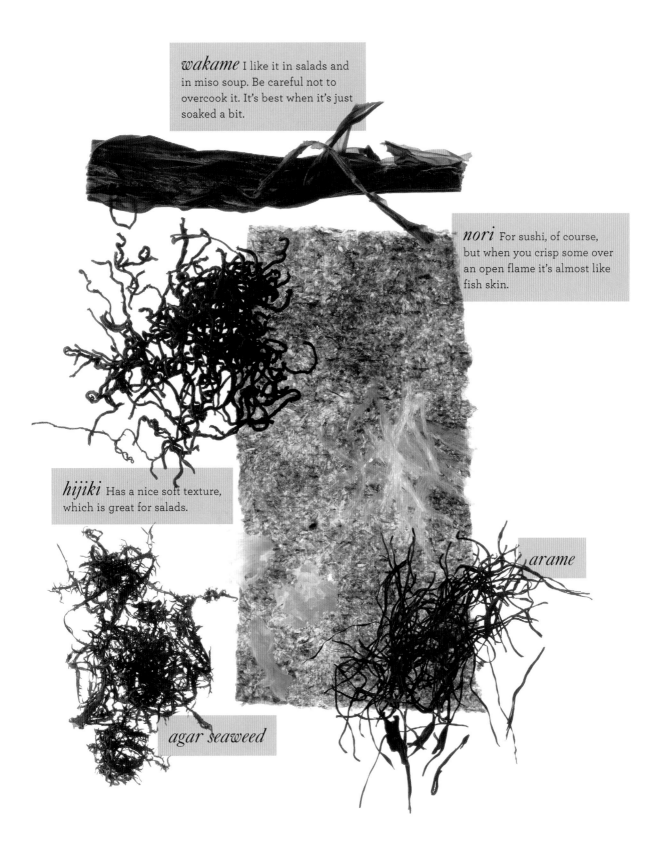

wakame I like it in salads and in miso soup. Be careful not to overcook it. It's best when it's just soaked a bit.

nori For sushi, of course, but when you crisp some over an open flame it's almost like fish skin.

hijiki Has a nice soft texture, which is great for salads.

arame

agar seaweed

cornmeal-crusted tempeh
with smoked tomato sauce, green chile relish, black bean puree, *and* braised kale

When I was living in L.A., I had access to all kinds of great chiles from Mexico, so I developed a few Southwestern dishes. I like this spicy sauce with the slight sweetness of cornmeal. This is a hearty entrée, down to the bean puree and the kale. If you want to tone down the spiciness, you can pull the chiles out of the sauce before you blend it.

For the tempeh:

8 tablespoons shoyu soy sauce
1-inch piece of fresh ginger, peeled and sliced ⅛ inch thick
2 garlic cloves, sliced
2 medium dried ancho chiles

2 medium dried chipotle chiles
1 large bay leaf
10 whole black peppercorns
2 (8-ounce) packages tempeh

For the tomato sauce:

Sea salt
4 tablespoons extra-virgin olive oil
1 large onion, diced
2 garlic cloves, minced
2 carrots, diced
1 celery stalk, diced

2 medium dried ancho chiles, stemmed
2 medium dried chipotle chiles, stemmed
2 (12-ounce) cans fire-roasted tomatoes, including juice
½ cup vegetable stock
3 tablespoons Earth Balance

For the black bean puree:

2 tablespoons olive oil
½ onion, finely diced
2 garlic cloves, minced
1 (15-ounce) can black beans, including liquid
Sea salt and freshly ground black pepper

For the green chile relish:

1 Anaheim chile
1 garlic clove, minced
1 shallot, minced
Salt and freshly ground black pepper to taste

To fry the tempeh and serve:

½ cup yellow cornmeal
Salt and freshly ground black pepper
¼ cup canola oil
Braised Kale (page 136)

1   *Make the tempeh:* In a large pot, combine the shoyu, ginger, garlic, chiles, bay leaf, peppercorns, and 6 cups water and bring to a boil. Cut each slab of tempeh on the bias into ¼-inch slices. Place the tempeh in the boiling broth, reduce the heat, and simmer for 45 minutes. Remove the tempeh with a slotted spoon to a plate and reserve the cooking liquid. Let cool.

2   *Make the tomato sauce:* Place a large sauté pan over medium heat. Sprinkle the bottom with a pinch of salt and heat for 1 minute. Add the oil and heat for 30 seconds, being careful not to let it smoke. This will create a nonstick effect. Add the onion and sauté for 3 minutes. Add the garlic, carrots, and celery and cook for 8 to 10 minutes, stirring occasionally, until softened and lightly browned. Add the chiles, tomatoes, and stock. Bring to a simmer and cook for 45 minutes.

3   Remove from the sauce and discard 1 ancho chile and 1 chipotle chile. Working in batches if necessary, pour the sauce into a blender, cover the lid with a towel (the hot liquid tends to erupt), and blend on high. Return the sauce to the pan and stir in the Earth Balance, 1 tablespoon at a time. Set aside, covered to keep warm.

4   *Make the black bean puree:* In a small pot over medium heat, heat the oil for 30 seconds. Add the onion and garlic and sauté, stirring frequently, until the onion is soft and translucent. Add the beans and their liquid, season with salt and pepper to taste, and cook, stirring occasionally, for 10 minutes. Place the beans in a food processor and pulse until pureed.

5   *Make the green chile relish:* Holding the chile with tongs, char over a gas burner until blackened, then peel, seed, and finely dice it. (Alternatively, put the chile on a baking sheet under a broiler and cook, turning, until blackened on all sides.) In a small bowl, combine the chile with the rest of the relish ingredients.

6   *Fry the tempeh and serve:* In a mixing bowl, combine the cornmeal with salt and pepper to taste. Dredge each piece of tempeh in the mixture, coating it well. Place a large sauté pan over medium heat. Sprinkle the bottom with a pinch of salt and heat for 1 minute. Add the oil and heat for 30 seconds, being careful not to let it smoke. Add the tempeh, in batches if necessary, and cook until well browned, 2 to 3 minutes on each side. Remove from the pan. Serve with the Braised Kale, black bean puree, tomato sauce, and green chile relish.

Makes 6 to 8 servings
Prep time: 2 hours

THE TEMPEH ARTISAN: Seth Tibbott

FOUNDER AND PRESIDENT, TURTLE ISLAND FOODS, HOOD RIVER, OR

Tempeh is an amazing soy-based protein that originated in ancient Indonesia and is still a big part of a typical Indonesian diet. Dense and flavorful, it satisfies the umami (savory) craving that meat-eaters get. Seth Tibbott, founder and president of Turtle Island Foods, is a rare breed— he makes tempeh using ancient methods, right here in the States.

TAL: We've all heard that tempeh is super-nutritious because it's fermented. Can you decode that for us?

SETH: The fermentation is where the magic happens—it breaks down the proteins and enzymes in the soybeans, making them easier to digest and assimilate. The fermentation process breaks down the oligosaccharides found in soybeans that are known for causing digestion problems.

T: What first inspired you to make tempeh?

S: Well, in 1977 I was living in Tennessee. Tempeh needs an 88-degree temperature to be perfect, which is just about the average temperature in Tennessee in July. That's when I made my first batch, and it was love at first bite.

T: And now you manufacture and package it?

S: Yes, but there are only really three tempeh makers of any size in the United States. So it's not like you can order tempeh equipment. You're always getting pasta and meat equipment and making it fit your needs.

T: Can you give us a quick explanation of how tempeh is made?

S: Sure. First the hull from the soybean is removed. Then the bean splits into halves naturally, and is either soaked overnight (that's how it's done in Indonesia) or cooked for an hour, then cooled and dried. Then a culture is added to the soybeans—we use *Rhizopus oligosporus*—but in Indonesia there are various molds used. Next the beans go into plastic bags that have little pinpoint holes every few inches (before plastic bags were available in Indonesia, it was banana leaves). The idea is to create this perfect little ecosystem—just the right temperature, just the right moisture level. It's tricky. Then the bags go into an incubator overnight, and the culture goes to work on the proteins. About 24 hours later, the beans have grown into this solid white cake that's knit together by thousands of yards of mycelia—the roots of the culture. At this point the tempeh has a fragrant, mushroomy smell and is solid like a paperback book. Then we steam it to pasteurize it, and vacuum seal it for the stores.

T: You've been to Indonesia to observe the process. What did you see there?

S: Well, over there tempeh is a cottage industry, under primitive, third-world conditions. Nothing you would do here—bamboo colanders, where we use stainless steel, for example. I saw tempeh incubating right out in the streets. It was amazing that such beautiful, white, firm tempeh could be made under those unsanitary conditions. Also, in Indonesia, tempeh is used within two or three days of being made, because without refrigeration it can't keep. People get it at the market, cook it, and eat it, whereas we don't really roll like that. So the challenge was to take this process and bring it to Western sanitary standards. Just getting that incubation and fermentation right is a real challenge. The book on processing is still being written.

"The fermentation is where the magic happens—it breaks down the proteins and enzymes in the soybeans, making them easier to digest and assimilate."

T: I usually don't feel like eating what I cook. After making tempeh for so many years, are you off it?

S: Really, it's still one of my favorite things. When you eat it, you just feel good. You feel like you're eating a wonder food.

Chapter

I don't really like to follow recipes, and with desserts you have to. So I turned to a friend to create the amazing desserts here. Some are fresh and light, others are rich and creamy—there's an array of wonderful options to top off any entrée in the book.

DESSERTS: Oven-Roasted Banana Rum Cheesecake with Spiced Pecan Crust and Maple Rum Sauce(p198) *Lemon Pistachio Cookies with Wild Blueberries*(p202) Black Pepper Shortcakes with Blackberry Basil Sauce and Cinnamon Cream(p204) *Seasonal Fruit in Papillote with Whipped Cashew Cream*(p206) Chocolate Chip Peanut Butter Cake with Berry Sorbet(p210) *Coffee Date Cake with Coconut Irish Cream Sauce*(p214) Tropical Tapioca Pudding(p216) *Vanilla Bean Panna Cotta with Orange Sauce*(p218) ✳

GUEST CHEF:
Serafina Magnussen

✳ *"Baking has a lot of science to it—it's not quite as free-form as cooking. The challenge of adapting desserts for a vegan diet is removing the butter and the eggs. But after playing with a couple of recipes, you develop a knack for using substitutions. I love Earth Balance for butter, and I know there's an unsalted version in the works. There's a plethora of milk substitutes. I lean toward nut milks rather than soy—people tend to eat so much soy already, and it's important nutritionally to have diversity. And I love using ground flaxseed instead of eggs— tons of nutrients there."*

My friend Serafina Magnussen, who has traveled all over the country with me as a sort of sous chef, is a wonder with sweets. She makes some of the best desserts I've ever had. A lot of vegan baked goods just don't taste good—they're lacking in texture or moisture. Serafina's are delicious. With a healthful approach and really clean ingredients, she makes fantastic treats that are satisfying, rich, and indulgent.

Chef Serafina Magnussen with Chef Tal

oven-roasted **banana rum cheesecake** *with* spiced pecan crust *and* maple rum sauce

A bunch of overripe bananas on the counter is a great excuse for whipping up this dessert. You want the skins to have a few brown spots—no green. It's the moisture of the extra-ripe bananas that makes for the traditional cheesecake texture.

For the oven-roasted bananas:

4 large, very ripe bananas

For the maple rum sauce:

1 cup grade B organic
    maple syrup
4 tablespoons Earth Balance
Sea salt
1 tablespoon dark rum

For the spiced pecan crust:

1 cup pecan nut flour (see note,
    page 201)
½ cup spelt flour (white or whole)
1 tablespoon firmly packed light
    brown sugar
4 tablespoons Earth Balance,
    partially melted
⅛ teaspoon ground cardamom
½ teaspoon ground ginger
Pinch of sea salt

For the filling:

16 ounces nondairy cream cheese
¾ cup firmly packed light brown sugar
¾ teaspoon ground cinnamon
¼ cup dark rum
2 tablespoons cornstarch
¼ teaspoon salt

To serve:

Toasted pecan halves

1   *Make the oven-roasted bananas:* Preheat the oven to 325°F. Place the unpeeled bananas on a roasting pan and roast in the center of the oven for 15 to 20 minutes, until the bananas are soft, the skins are dark brown, and some juice is seeping out. Let the bananas cool to room temperature in the pan in their skins. Set aside. Increase the oven temperature to 400°F.

2   *Make the maple rum sauce:* In a small saucepan, combine the maple syrup, Earth Balance, and salt to taste and bring to a boil over medium-high heat. Reduce the heat to medium-low and simmer, stirring frequently, until the sauce has thickened slightly, about 10 minutes.

3   Remove from the heat and add the rum, stirring well; be careful, as the sauce will bubble up a bit. Let cool for a few minutes, then taste and add more salt if necessary. Cool to room temperature, then transfer to a squeeze bottle. The sauce can be rewarmed by putting the bottle in a pan of hot water off the heat.

4   *Make the spiced pecan crust:* Combine all the crust ingredients in a bowl and stir until well incorporated. Press the crust into a 9-inch springform pan and put in the freezer for 5 minutes. Bake in the center of the oven for 8 to 10 minutes, until the crust looks a little dry and the edges are light golden. Remove to a wire rack to cool completely.

5   *Make the filling:* Peel the roasted bananas and remove any obvious strings. In a food processor, puree the bananas until very smooth. Add the remaining ingredients and pulse until smooth, scraping the sides of the bowl periodically; do not overprocess, or the cream cheese will separate and curdle.

6   Pour the filling into the crust and bake on the center rack of the oven for 10 minutes. Reduce the oven temperature to 350°F and bake for another 35 to 45 minutes, until the top is the color of light brown sugar and the center of the cheesecake is set but still jiggles slightly; a toothpick inserted into the center should come out clean.

7   Let the cheesecake cool to room temperature on a rack for at least 1 hour, then cover with plastic wrap and chill in the refrigerator for at least 3 hours, preferably overnight.

8   *To serve:* Rewarm the sauce in a pan of hot water. Use an offset spatula or a thin knife to loosen the edges of the cheesecake, remove the sides of the pan, and cut the cake into slices. Serve with the warm sauce and toasted pecans.

Makes 6 to 8 servings
Prep time: 1 hour, 50 minutes, plus 3 hours chilling

> **MAKING NUT FLOUR:**
> *To make your own nut flour, first freeze raw nuts overnight. Place about 1 cup of the frozen nuts in a food processor at a time and pulse until finely ground. Freezing the nuts prevents them from turning to nut butter in the food processor as the blade heats up—but be warned, it will be loud!*

lemon pistachio cookies *with* wild blueberries

This simple recipe is open to endless variation. You can substitute any other nut flour for the pistachio flour, use other dried fruits, or substitute another citrus zest for the lemon. I find Ener-G brand to be the best egg replacer for cookies; it's made from potato starch. This recipe takes some advance planning. If you don't have pistachio flour on hand, you can freeze the nuts to make your own.

½ cup firmly packed light brown sugar
¼ cup granulated sugar
Zest of 2 lemons, preferably Meyer lemons
1 cup pistachio nut flour
  (see note, page 201)
1 cup whole spelt flour
1 tablespoon cornstarch

½ teaspoon salt
1 teaspoon baking soda
8 tablespoons Earth Balance
1½ teaspoons Ener-G egg replacer
1 teaspoon lemon extract
½ cup dried wild blueberries

1 Combine the sugars and lemon zest in an airtight container. Stir well with a fork, cover, and set aside to infuse for about 4 hours.

2 Preheat the oven to 350°F. Line two baking sheets with parchment paper.

3 In a food processor, combine ¾ cup of the pistachio flour, the spelt flour, cornstarch, salt, and baking soda and process to combine and to grind the pistachios to a finer powder. Set aside.

4 In a large mixing bowl, use an electric mixer to cream the sugar mixture and Earth Balance for about 2 minutes, until smooth and fluffy. In a small bowl, whisk together the egg replacer and 2 tablespoons water. Add the egg replacer mixture along with the lemon extract to the sugar mixture and scrape the sides of the bowl well. Mix for 1 to 2 minutes, until well combined.

5 Scrape the sides of the bowl again, then add the flour mixture. Mix on low speed until just combined. The dough will be slightly sticky. Fold in the blueberries.

6 Scoop out tablespoonfuls of dough, roll into 1-inch balls, then roll the balls in the remaining ¼ cup pistachio flour. Place on the prepared baking sheets 1½ inches apart and press down to flatten slightly.

7 Bake for 14 to 16 minutes, until lightly browned at the edges but still soft in the center, rotating the pans halfway through. (For a super-crisp cookie, bake a few minutes longer.) Let cool on the pans for 5 minutes, then transfer to wire racks to cool completely.

Makes 2 dozen cookies
Prep time: 30 minutes, plus 4 hours infusing

black pepper shortcakes
with blackberry basil sauce *and* cinnamon cream

This is a pretty dessert with a vegan version of whipped cream that's fantastic. If you can find Thai basil or cinnamon basil, use that in the sauce. They're both incredible with blackberries.

For the blackberry basil sauce:

6 cups fresh blackberries, or
   2 (12-ounce) bags frozen blackberries
½ teaspoon freshly squeezed lemon
   juice, or more to taste

Pinch of sea salt
1 sprig fresh basil
1 tablespoon light agave
   nectar, or to taste

For the black pepper shortcakes:

3 cups white spelt flour, plus more
   for dusting
1 tablespoon baking powder
½ cup plus 2 tablespoons granulated sugar
¼ teaspoon salt

1 tablespoon freshly ground black pepper
7 tablespoons very cold Earth Balance,
   cut into ½-inch cubes
1 cup plain unsweetened soy creamer,
   plus more for brushing

To serve:

Whipped Cashew Cream (page 26; add ½ teaspoon ground cinnamon with the vanilla)

1   *Make the blackberry basil sauce:* Place half of the blackberries, the lemon juice, salt, and basil sprig in a small saucepan and bring to a simmer over medium heat. Cook, stirring frequently to break up the berries, for about 8 minutes, until the berries are soft and broken down.

2   Remove from the heat and let steep for at least 20 minutes, up to overnight. Remove and discard the basil, then pour the sauce into a blender. Puree, then sweeten to taste with the agave nectar and add more lemon juice if needed.

3   Push the sauce through a fine-mesh sieve back into the saucepan and gently fold in the remaining whole blackberries. When ready to serve, heat over low heat just until the sauce

is warm and the berries are thawed (if using frozen). Alternatively, chill the sauce in the refrigerator, covered, and serve cold.

4   *Make the black pepper shortcakes:* Preheat the oven to 425°F. Line a baking sheet with parchment paper. Sift the flour and baking powder into a large mixing bowl, then stir in the ½ cup sugar, the salt, and pepper. Scatter the Earth Balance into the flour and, using a pastry cutter, a fork, or—the best tool—your hands, cut the Earth Balance into the flour until the largest chunks are the size of large peas.

5   Make a well in the center of the mixture and add the creamer; using your hands or a wooden spoon, gently stir to make a soft, somewhat sticky dough, being careful not to overwork. Turn the dough out onto a floured work surface and pat it out to 1 inch thick. Using a biscuit cutter, cut the dough into 2½-inch rounds and place 1½ inches apart on the prepared baking sheet. Gently press the scraps together and cut out more rounds. Brush the tops of the rounds with creamer and sprinkle with the remaining 2 tablespoons sugar.

6   Bake in the middle of the oven until golden brown, about 12 minutes, rotating the pan 180 degrees halfway through. Remove to a wire rack to cool. Serve the shortcakes with warm or chilled blackberry basil sauce and top with the Whipped Cashew Cream.

Makes 8 servings
Prep time: 45 minutes

seasonal fruit *in* papillote *with* whipped cashew cream

This is one of the simplest desserts to make, and it's a brilliant way to showcase whatever's in season. You just toss ripe fruit with a few herbs and spices, sprinkle on some sweetener, add a pat of nondairy butter, and bake in parchment paper for a few minutes. Papillotes can be made as individual dessert pockets or larger, to share family-style at the table. You can use your imagination in choosing which flavors to put together. There really aren't any rules, but here are a few no-fail combinations.

Spring and Summer:

* strawberries with vanilla bean and orange zest
* raspberries and mango slices with fresh ginger and mint
* nectarines and peaches with fresh basil and cinnamon
* pitted cherries and apricots with vanilla bean and balsamic vinegar
* blueberries and peaches with lemon zest, fresh thyme, and mint

Fall and Winter:

* figs and pears with lemon zest, vanilla bean, and balsamic vinegar
* apples, pears, and dates with cinnamon, nutmeg, cloves, and ginger
* pears and quince with black pepper and red wine vinegar
* bananas, kiwis, and pineapple with ginger, star anise, and vanilla bean
* persimmons and grapes with lemon zest and cinnamon

For each single-serving papillote:

Parchment paper
1 tablespoon Earth Balance
1½ cups pitted, peeled, and sliced
   (if necessary) fruit
Pinch of sea salt
1 teaspoon freshly squeezed lemon
   juice or vinegar

Spices (see list on page 208; optional)
1 to 2 tablespoons sweetener such as
   brown sugar, maple syrup, light or
   amber agave nectar, cane sugar, honey
   (if you use it), or raw sugar
1 sprig fresh herb, or more to taste
   (see list on page 208; optional)

To serve:

Whipped Cashew Cream (page 26)

❋ custom options: more herbs and spices to choose from:

1 small sprig fresh thyme, basil, cilantro, tarragon, chervil,
     or mint, or more if the herb is delicately flavored
¼ vanilla bean, split and seeds scraped, or ¼ teaspoon
     vanilla bean paste
⅛ teaspoon ground cinnamon, or 1 (1-inch) stick cinnamon
Pinch of freshly grated nutmeg
1 whole clove, or a pinch of ground cloves
1 teaspoon whole coriander seeds
5 juniper berries
1 whole cardamom pod, or a pinch of ground cardamom
1 whole star anise
Pinch of ground allspice
⅛ teaspoon ground ginger, or 2 slices fresh ginger
1 teaspoon cocoa nibs
1 tablespoon whole black peppercorns, or ¼ teaspoon
     freshly ground black pepper
A few threads of saffron
Pinch of ground cayenne or other dried chile

1. Preheat the oven to 450°F. For each single-serving papillote, cut a piece of parchment paper 10 inches square, fold it in half, and trim it into a wide semicircle, cutting close to the cut edges of the paper. Unfold the parchment and place the Earth Balance in the center next to the fold.

2. In a medium bowl, combine the fruit, salt, lemon juice, spices (if using), and sweetener and toss to combine.

3. Pile the fruit on top of and around the Earth Balance, keeping near the center of the parchment. Scrape the bowl well to get all the spices and sweetener onto the fruit. Lay the herb sprig (if using) on top.

4. Fold the parchment over the fruit and seal the edges: Starting at one end, fold a small section ¼ inch in toward the center, fold over again, and crease well; continue to fold and crease the edges until the whole parchment is sealed with a firm, final crease at the other end. Place on a baking sheet and bake in the upper third of the oven for 7 minutes.

5. Using a large spatula, transfer the papillote to a serving plate, and cut the parchment open in the center, being careful to stay clear of the steam—it's hot!

6. Dollop a little Whipped Cashew Cream in the center, and place a heaping spoonful on the side for dipping. Serve immediately, and if you've used whole spices, warn your guests that they are not to be eaten.

Makes 1 single-serving papillote
Prep time: 30 minutes (for 4 papillotes)

chocolate chip peanut butter cake *with* berry sorbet

This is one of those recipes that uses ground flaxseeds to replace eggs. It's best to buy the seeds whole and grind them yourself—you can dedicate a coffee grinder to spices and seeds, if you like (not the same one you use for coffee). A tiny whisk is good for whipping flaxseeds, but even better is a small, round, battery-powered whisk used for frothing milk. Any type of nut, soy, or oat milk works here, but don't use rice milk, which is much thinner.

2¼ cups white spelt flour or
    unbleached all-purpose flour
1½ cups firmly packed dark
    brown sugar
1 cup chunky all-natural
    peanut butter
½ cup cold Earth Balance
Pinch of sea salt

2 tablespoons ground flaxseeds
1 cup hazelnut milk
2 teaspoons baking powder
½ teaspoon baking soda
2 teaspoons vanilla extract
½ cup vegan semisweet
    chocolate chips

To serve:

Berry Sorbet (recipe follows)

1   Preheat the oven to 350°F. Lightly grease a 10-inch square pan. (If you don't have one, use a 9-inch pan and bake a couple of minutes longer.) In a large bowl using an electric mixer, combine the flour, brown sugar, peanut butter, Earth Balance, and salt, blending at low speed until the mixture forms fine crumbs. Reserve 1 cup of the crumbs for the topping and set aside.

2   In a small bowl, with a small whisk, whip the flaxseeds with ⅓ cup water until frothy. The mixture should resemble egg whites in texture. Add the whipped flaxseeds, hazelnut milk, baking powder, baking soda, and vanilla to the crumb mixture. Stir well to combine, but do not overwork.

3   Transfer the batter to the prepared pan, smoothing the top, and sprinkle with the reserved crumb mixture. Sprinkle with the chocolate chips. Bake in the center of the oven for 25 to 30 minutes, until a toothpick inserted into the center of the cake comes out clean.

4   Let cool to room temperature, then cut; serve with the Berry Sorbet.

Makes about 12 servings
Prep time: 45 minutes

For the chocolate chip peanut butter cake:

❋ berry **sorbet**

Make the base; let it chill as long as possible, preferably overnight, to intensify the flavors, then freeze in the ice cream maker 2 to 3 hours before serving. The amount of agave you use can vary, depending on how sweet the fruit is. Adjust as your palate desires; just remember that flavors tend to mellow after freezing.

2 (16-ounce) bags frozen berries
(strawberries, raspberries, blackberries, blueberries, or a combination), defrosted in the bags
¾ cup agave nectar, or to taste
Pinch of sea salt
3 tablespoons freshly squeezed lemon juice
(add less if your fruit is very tart)

Put the berries and their liquid, along with 1 cup water, the agave nectar, and salt in a blender and puree until well blended.

Taste, then add the lemon juice and more agave nectar, if desired; blend again briefly to combine.

Strain the mixture through a fine-mesh sieve to remove the seeds. You should have about 4 cups strained fruit liquid. Taste again, and adjust the sweetness and lemon juice if necessary.

Pour into a covered container and refrigerate for at least 2 hours, preferably overnight.

Freeze in an ice cream maker according to the manufacturer's instructions. Transfer to the freezer to firm up if necessary, and let the sorbet sit at room temperature for about 10 minutes to soften before serving.

Makes about 1 quart

For the coffee date cake:

coconut irish cream sauce

This is my vegan version of Bailey's Irish Cream liqueur, without the whiskey. Of course, you can add a good Irish whiskey or Scotch and pour over ice for an amazing cocktail, but the sauce is scrumptious without it. Diamond brand chocolate almond milk is excellent, and you can heat the rest for some marvelous hot chocolate.

2 teaspoons tapioca starch or cornstarch
1 (13½-ounce) can coconut milk (not light)
½ cup chocolate almond milk
¼ cup firmly packed dark brown sugar
½ teaspoon unsweetened cocoa powder

Combine the tapioca starch and 2 teaspoons water in a small bowl and stir to make a slurry. Set aside.

In a medium saucepan, whisk together the coconut milk, almond milk, brown sugar, and cocoa powder. Bring to a low boil, whisking occasionally, over medium-high heat.

When the mixture is gently boiling, add the slurry and whisk vigorously to combine well. Simmer for 2 minutes, then remove from the heat.

Cool for a few minutes, then pour through a fine-mesh sieve into a container or squeeze bottle and cover; a skin may form on the surface, but a vigorous shake or straining will easily remove it.

Reheat by placing the container in a bowl of hot water until warm, and shake vigorously before serving.

Makes about 2 cups

coffee date cake *with* coconut irish cream sauce

This is a moist cake, flavored with coffee. Fresh, soft dates are a must. Use the variety you like best; Medjool, Halaway, and honey dates all work. To make sticky dates easier to chop, freeze them overnight, then slice them open and remove the pits. Toss the dates in your food processor and pulse until chopped. For this recipe, the date pieces should be relatively small. If you don't have coffee extract, brew a cup of extremely strong coffee (think rich espresso), let it cool, and use that instead.

2 cups white spelt flour
1½ teaspoons baking powder
½ teaspoon sea salt
1½ cups firmly packed chopped
  pitted dates
1½ teaspoons baking soda

5 tablespoons Earth Balance
½ cup firmly packed dark
  brown sugar
2 tablespoons ground flaxseeds
5 teaspoons coffee extract

To serve:

Coconut Irish Cream Sauce (page 213)
Whipped Cashew Cream (page 26)
Pitted dates, halved

1   Preheat the oven to 375°F. Grease the bottom and sides of a 9-inch square cake pan and dust with flour. Sift the flour, baking powder, and salt together into a medium bowl and set aside.

2   In a medium saucepan, bring 2 cups water to a boil, keeping covered to prevent evaporation. Add the dates and simmer over medium heat for 5 minutes, stirring occasionally. Remove from the heat, add the baking soda, and stir to combine; the mixture will be fizzy and bubble up a bit. Stir well to incorporate. Let the date mixture sit for 20 minutes, uncovered (the baking soda breaks down the fiber of the dates).

3   In a large bowl using an electric mixer, cream the Earth Balance and brown sugar until well incorporated and fluffy, scraping the sides of the bowl often. In a small bowl, with a small whisk, whip the flaxseeds with ⅓ cup water until frothy. The mixture should resemble egg whites in texture. Add the whipped flaxseeds to the brown sugar mixture and mix on medium speed until well blended. Add the coffee extract to the dates and stir to combine.

4   Add the date mixture, alternating with the flour mixture, to the brown sugar mixture, starting with the dates, mixing well but gently between each addition until all ingredients are incorporated. Do not overmix.

5   Pour the batter into the prepared pan and bake for 25 to 30 minutes, until a toothpick inserted in the center comes out clean and the surface of the cake springs back when gently pressed. Let cool for 15 minutes, then cut into squares. Drizzle each square with some of the Coconut Irish Cream Sauce, dollop with Whipped Cashew Cream, and top with 2 date halves. Serve warm.

Makes 6 to 8 servings
Prep time: 1 hour

tropical tapioca pudding

This dessert is really about the rich flavor of the coconut milk and the natural sweetness of the fruits—it's not supersweet. You can use one of the tropical fruits listed or create your own combination, and feel free to play with the proportions—you might want to include extra fruit or, if your sweet tooth demands it, a bit more sugar.

For the tapioca pudding:

2 (13½-ounce) cans coconut milk (not light)
½ cup small pearl tapioca (not instant)
½ teaspoon sea salt
½ cup granulated sugar, or ¼ cup light agave nectar
1 teaspoon vanilla bean paste or vanilla extract

Tropical fruit (choose one or combine):

2 large ripe bananas, diced
1 ripe mango, diced
1 to 1½ cups drained canned crushed
    pineapple or pineapple chunks
1 to 1½ cups pomegranate seeds
1 large persimmon, diced
3 or 4 kiwis, peeled and diced or sliced

1   Combine the coconut milk (be sure to scrape all the thick cream from the cans), 1 full
    can of water, the tapioca, and salt in a medium saucepan. Bring to a boil over medium-
    high heat, stirring frequently to prevent sticking.

2   Stir in the sugar, then reduce the heat to medium-low and bring to a gentle simmer.
    Cook, stirring frequently, until the pudding has thickened and the tapioca pearls are
    completely translucent, 20 to 25 minutes.

3   Remove from the heat and stir in the vanilla bean paste. Gently fold in the fruit and let
    cool for 15 minutes. Spoon into serving bowls and serve warm, or chill, covered, in the
    refrigerator for 2 hours before serving. Garnish with your favorite fresh fruit.

Makes 8 to 10 servings
Prep time: 50 minutes, plus 2 hours chilling if desired

vanilla bean panna cotta
with orange sauce

Here's a play on the classic vanilla-and-orange Creamsicle, with the addition of a crunchy brittle. Definitely use a real vanilla bean or vanilla bean paste for this dessert, because the seeds make the panna cotta look elegant and won't darken it like vanilla extract would. Make the panna cotta first and while it's chilling you can make the brittle. As the brittle cools, you can make the sauce.

For the panna cotta:

1½ teaspoons agar-agar flakes
⅓ cup boiling water
1½ cups thick Cashew Cream (page 26) thinned with water to the consistency of whole milk (about ¾ cup thick cream and ¾ cup water)

1 cup plain unsweetened almond milk
½ cup granulated sugar
⅛ teaspoon sea salt
½ vanilla bean, split and seeds scraped, or 1 tablespoon vanilla bean paste

For the orange sauce:

1 cup freshly squeezed orange juice
1 tablespoon grated orange zest
3 tablespoons firmly packed light brown sugar
4 tablespoons Earth Balance
¼ teaspoon sea salt
2 tablespoons Grand Marnier or other orange liqueur

To serve:

About 1 cup Rosemary Pine Nut Brittle in large chunks (recipe follows)

1   *Make the panna cotta:* Put the agar-agar in a small bowl and pour the boiling water over them; let soak for 5 minutes.

2   In a medium saucepan, combine the Cashew Cream, almond milk, sugar, salt, and soaked agar-agar. If using the vanilla bean, add it now, with the scraped seeds. Place the pan over medium-high heat and bring to a simmer, whisking constantly and watching to make sure it doesn't boil over. As soon as a foam starts to rise up in the pan, reduce the heat to low. Simmer for 3 minutes. Remove from the heat. If using vanilla bean paste, add it now.

3   Pour the mixture through a fine-mesh sieve into 6 (1-cup) ramekins. Let cool to room temperature, then chill in the refrigerator for 2 to 3 hours, until set.

4   *Make the orange sauce:* In a small saucepan, combine the orange juice and zest, brown sugar, Earth Balance, and salt. Bring to a boil over medium-high heat, stirring occasionally. Reduce the heat to medium-low and simmer until thickened slightly and reduced by half, about 15 minutes.

5   Remove from the heat, stir in the liqueur, then pour through a fine-mesh sieve into a heatproof container or squeeze bottle. If not using right away, let the sauce cool to room temperature, then refrigerate for up to 2 days. Reheat by placing the container in a pan of hot water.

6   *To serve:* Run a thin knife or small offset spatula around the edges of the ramekins to loosen the panna cotta. Place a serving plate over the top of each ramekin and turn over. Gently tap the ramekin; the panna cotta should slide out easily. Drizzle or squeeze some of the orange sauce over the panna cotta and top with a few pieces of the nut brittle. Serve immediately.

Makes 6 servings
Prep time: 45 minutes, plus 2 to 3 hours chilling

rosemary pine nut **brittle**

You'll need a candy thermometer for this brittle; the caramel heats up fairly quickly, and it's critical that you keep an eye on the temperature. Be careful whenever you're making caramel because it gets extremely hot and can be dangerous. This recipe makes more than you'll need to top the panna cotta, but that's good. It's a great dessert all by itself.

1 cup granulated sugar
2 tablespoons Earth Balance
1 tablespoon light agave nectar
1 teaspoon sea salt

1 cup pine nuts, toasted
2 teaspoons minced
   fresh rosemary

Line a baking sheet with aluminum foil. In a 1½- to 2-quart saucepan, gently stir together the sugar and ¼ cup water.

Add the Earth Balance and agave nectar to the pan and bring to a boil over medium-high heat, stirring to combine. Attach the candy thermometer to the side of the pan, and do not stir once the mixture is boiling.

Increase the heat slightly and cook until the mixture is a golden caramel color and the thermometer reads 350°F. Remove from the heat and, using a nonstick heat-resistant spatula, immediately stir in the salt, pine nuts, and rosemary. Quickly but carefully, pour the mixture into the prepared pan, spreading so that the nuts are in a single layer.

Let cool to room temperature, about 1 hour, then break into chunks and store in an airtight container at room temperature for up to 1 week. Do not refrigerate, as this will cause the sugar to melt.

Makes about 2 cups

my favorite

SEASONAL
DINNER PARTY
MENUS

One of the best things about cooking for friends is putting together a menu that feels fun and right for the time of year. Seasonal cooking is, of course, largely about available ingredients, but it's also about mood, responding to how people are feeling and what they might be craving—not just their mouths but their spirits. Here are some combinations I like, culled from the recipes in this book.

MENUS: Orange, Belgian Endive, and Quinoa Salad with Champagne Vinaigrette *Artichoke Ricotta Tortellini with Saffron Cream Sauce* Vanilla Bean Panna Cotta with Orange Sauce *Cream of Asparagus Soup* Gardein "Chicken" Scaloppini with Shiitake Sake Sauce, Braised Pea Shoots, and Crispy Udon Noodle Cakes *Tropical Tapioca Pudding* Heirloom Tomato Salad with Crisped Capers *Old Bay Tofu Cakes with Pan-Roasted Summer Vegetables, Horseradish Cream, Apples, and Beets* Black Pepper Shortcakes with Blackberry Basil Sauce and Cinnamon Cream *Celery Root Soup with Granny Smith Apples* Peppercorn-Encrusted Portobello Fillets with Yellow Tomato Béarnaise and Mashed Potatoes *Oven-Roasted Banana Rum Cheesecake with Spiced Pecan Crust and Maple Rum Sauce* ✳

A WINTER DINNER

SALAD

orange, belgian endive, *and* quinoa salad *with* champagne vinaigrette 74

ENTRÉE

artichoke ricotta tortellini *with* saffron cream sauce 164

DESSERT

vanilla bean panna cotta *with* orange sauce 218

※ *This meal starts with something light and refreshing—a wintry citrus salad—and then moves into cozy comfort food. I love a rich dish, like this tortellini, on a cold night. It's the kind of thing people love to tuck into in winter and might find too heavy other times of the year. Serve a Pinot Grigio or a Chardonnay with these dishes. Dessert here is lush and satisfying.*

A SPRING DINNER

SOUP

cream *of* asparagus soup   96

ENTRÉE

gardein "chicken" scaloppini *with*   154
shiitake sake sauce, braised pea shoots,
and crispy udon noodle cakes

DESSERT

tropical tapioca pudding   216

Asparagus is one of my favorite signs of spring, and the color of this soup looks so fresh. The pea tendrils in the scaloppini are another seasonal touch. For a drink, sake might be nice, because it's in the sauce. The tropical tapioca pudding is really nimble—you can use whatever fruit you want. So it can be a transition from winter to spring, mixing whatever berries are available with winter fruits like citrus and mangoes.

A SUMMER DINNER

SALAD

heirloom tomato salad *with* crisped capers — 60

ENTRÉE

old bay tofu cakes *with* pan-roasted summer vegetables, horseradish cream, apples, *and* beets — 138

DESSERT

black pepper shortcakes *with* blackberry basil sauce *and* cinnamon cream — 204

* *This is an elegant meal with a summer-casual vibe. It's colorful and cheery, and nothing has to be served piping hot—perfect for a buffet or for dining outside. No matter where you live, local tomatoes are great in August. There's nothing like them, so I use them a couple of ways in this menu. Lots of the other components—fresh corn, basil, and blackberries—can come from your green market too, one of the great joys of summer cooking. A nice Pinot Noir would complement all these dishes.*

A FALL DINNER

SOUP

celery root soup *with* granny smith apples 100

ENTRÉE

peppercorn-encrusted portobello fillets *with* yellow tomato béarnaise *and* mashed potatoes 142

DESSERT

oven-roasted banana rum cheesecake *with* spiced pecan crust *and* maple rum sauce 198

✳ *As the weather gets cool, people crave heartier food, like a meaty, heavily sauced mushroom dish; the entrée here is almost like a roast. And it takes advantage of those last delicious tomatoes of the season. Serve it with a Chardonnay. The soup is a natural here—root vegetables and apples are both so autumnal. Imagine the fragrance of the maple rum sauce as you bring out dessert: It smells like fall.*

EATING
seasonally

I went to a small culinary school in New York called The Natural Gourmet Institute for Health & Culinary Arts, a school that focused on classic French cooking, but with an emphasis on local, organic, and seasonal ingredients. Cooking with the seasons is really a pleasure. You look forward to things as they come—spring asparagus, summer tomatoes, dark leafy greens in fall—and enjoy them when they taste best. In warmer places, of course, seasonality is not really an issue—you can get a vast array of fresh local produce anytime. For the rest of us, here are some of the green-market treats to look forward to at different times of the year. If you're not sure where your nearest farmers' market is, find it here: localharvest.org/farmers-markets.

what's in season when:

✳ SPRING

asparagus, beets, cabbage, cauliflower, cherries, cucumbers, fennel, fiddlehead ferns, greens, peas, peppers, radishes, raspberries, rhubarb, spinach, strawberries

✳ SUMMER

arugula, blackberries, blueberries, broccoli, cantaloupe, celery, cherries, corn, eggplant, gooseberries, grapes, green beans, kohlrabi, nectarines, peaches, pears, plums, potatoes, sugar snap peas, tomatoes, watermelon, zucchini

✳ FALL

apples, beans, cabbage, carrots, cauliflower, celery root, chard, chestnuts, collards, parsnips, pumpkins, summer squash, sweet potatoes, turnips, watercress

✳ WINTER

beets, brussels sprouts, celery, kale, mushrooms, radishes, turnips, winter squash

my favorite

VEGAN RESTAURANTS

There's fine vegan food popping up all over the United States.
Here are the restaurants I love to visit whenever I can.

UPSCALE FAVORITES

1 **Sublime**
1431 N. Federal Hwy.
Fort Lauderdale, FL 33304
954.539.9000
sublimeveg.com

2 **Madeleine Bistro**
18621 Ventura Blvd.
Tarzana, CA 91356
818.758.6971
madeleinebistro.com

3 **Millennium**
580 Geary St.
San Francisco, CA 94102
415.345.3900
millenniumrestaurant.com

4 **Sage's Café**
473 E. Broadway
Salt Lake City, UT 84111
801.322.3790
sagescafe.com

5 **Horizons**
611 S. 7th St.
Philadelphia, PA 19147
215.923.6117
horizonsphiladelphia.com

6 **Dragonfly**
247 King Ave.
Columbus, OH 43201
614.298.9986
dragonflyneov.com

7 **VegiTerranean**
21 Furnace St.
Akron, Ohio 44308
330.374.5550
thevegiterranean.com

8 **Candle 79**
154 E. 79th St.
New York, NY 10021
212.537.7179
candle79.com

CASUAL FAVORITES

9 **Native Foods**
(several locations in CA,
nativefoods.com)

10 **Candle Cafe**
1307 Third Ave.
New York, NY 10021
212.472.0970
candlecafe.com

11 **Veggie Grill**
(several locations in CA,
veggiegrill.com)

12 **Flore**
3818 W. Sunset Blvd.
Los Angeles, CA 90026
323.953.0611
florevegan.com

13 **The Chicago Diner**
3411 N. Halsted St.
Chicago, IL 60657
773.935.6696
veggiediner.com

COOKING GRAINS & BEANS:

cooking whole grains

The cooking times below are just a guide and can vary a bit depending on your stove and the pot you use.

GRAIN (1 cup dry)	WATER or STOCK NEEDED	COOKING TIME (minutes)
Barley, pear	3 cups	40 – 50
Barley, whole (hulled)	3 cups	60 – 75
Buckwheat	2 cups	15 – 20
Millet	2½ – 3 cups	18 – 25
Oats	2 – 2½ cups	15 – 25
Quinoa	2 cups	12 – 15
Rice, brown basmati	2 cups	35 – 45
Rice, brown short-grain	2 cups	40 – 50
Rice, brown long-grain	2 cups	40 – 50
Rice, wild	3 cups	45 – 60

Rinse grains before cooking. Then combine the grain and cooking water (or stock), bring to a boil, reduce heat to low, and simmer, covered, for the specified time. About 5 minutes before the cooking time is up, check for doneness. When done, remove from heat and let stand, covered, for 5 minutes.

cooking beans

BEAN	COOKING TIME (minutes)
Black beans	60 – 90
Black-eyed peas	45 – 60
Cannellini beans	60 – 90
Chickpeas	90 – 120
Kidney beans	90 – 120
Lentils, brown/green	30 – 40
Lentils, French	35 – 45
Lentils, red	15 – 25
Navy beans	90 – 120
Split peas	40 – 60

Most beans should be soaked before cooking (lentils and split peas are exceptions)—it shortens the cooking time and makes them easier to digest. You can soak beans overnight or do a quick version. Either way, first rinse the beans and remove any dirt, stones, or particles. To soak overnight, cover the beans with water and let sit for at least 6 hours.

To quick soak, cover the beans with water in a pot and bring to a boil. Let boil for 5 minutes, then remove from the heat, cover, and let sit for 1 hour. Drain the beans and rinse again.

To cook beans, combine 3 parts water to 1 part beans in a large pot. Bring to a boil, then reduce the heat and simmer, partially covered, until tender, using the chart above as a timing guide.

index:

thanks

to all the people who
contributed so much to this book:

Lia Ronnen, Robyn Wesley, Danielle Claro, Charlie Melcher,
Lauren Nathan, and everyone at Melcher Media, Mary Ellen
O'Neill and the team at HarperCollins, Serafina Magnussen,
Kathy Freston, Scot Jones, Joel Testa, Chad Sarno, Linda Long,
David Anderson, Yves Potvin, Clare Thomson, Larry Goldstein,
Liana Krisoff, David Cooper, air-conditioned, Hikari,
and everyone at California Specialty Farms

Thanks also to my family, friends, and colleagues for their support:

Cem Akin, Nanci Alexander, Ron and Patty Allison, Stein Amland, Dave and Molly Anderson, Scott Anderson, Paul Anthony, Adili Armon, Darrell Askey, Kirk Bachmann, Jason Baker, Sue Baker, Susan Baldassano, Josh Balk, Murray Bancroft, Dr. Barnard, Master Chef Brad Barnes, Dale Bartlet, Jack Bartlet, Steve Bashel, Kristina Beckman, Ryan Bennett, Ken Bergeron, Corey Berrien, Carla Bird, Greg Blake, Rob Bleifer, Jay Books, Alex Borja, Kevin Boylan, Lisa Boyman, Anthony Brown, Merle Brown, Bugambilia International, the team at Candle 79: Benay, Joy, Bart, Angel, Jorge, and all the staff; Elizabeth Castoria, Paul Chetirkin, Sophie Chiche, P.J. Chmiel, Michelle Cho, Craig Cochran, Joe Connelly, Amy Cook, Mark A. Costello, Fran Costigan, Tabitha M. Croscut, Novona Cruz, Ellen DeGeneres and Portia de Rossi, Emily Deschanel, Michael Dubanewicz, Chef Kevin Dunn, Dan Duplain, Bonnie Eldon, Lisa Erspamer, Scott Evens, Keith Ferrazzi, Melanie Ferreira, Rebecca Fisher, Derek Flynn, the team at Follow Your Heart: Dale, Corina, Marika, and Booth; Frank Forino, Kate Forte, Jorja Fox, Rory Freedman, Tom Freston, Melanie Friedlander, Bruce Friedrich, Front of the House, Massimo Galeano, Kara Gastin, Bob Goldberg, Ido Goldberg, Charlie Granquist, Bob Green, Urania Green, Mathew Griffith, Jill Gusman, Rhea Harris, Chris Hill, Colleen Holland, Mike and Suzi Hornbeek, Arianna Huffington, Chef Andrew Hunter, Chrissie Hynde, Beverly Kearney, Jay Kelly, Chris Kerr, Joan Kim, Percy Kleinops, Karla Koebernick, Andre Kroecher, Lisa Lange, the Lange family, Heinz Lauer, Kelvin Lee, Sherman Levey, Karen Logue, Kim Lorenz, Mark Mace, the team at Madeleine Bistro: Joe, Marcos, and the amazing staff; Mike Markarian, Jenny Mathau, Ko Matsumoto, Mary Max, Joe McCanta, Angelique McFarland, Peter McGoldrick, Erica Meier, Shelby Meizlik, George Mew, Libby Moore, Chef Dennis Moreland, Chris Moulson, Jessica R. Murray, George and Pam Myers, Ingrid Newkirk, Vince Nichols, Morgan Nims, Marie Oser, Wayne Pacelle, Ken Penn, Craig Peralta, Steve Perkins, Greg Peterman, Jeremy Peterson, Tanya Petrovna, Ron Pickarski, T.K. Pillan, Johanne Pillon, Jo Marie Pinto, Louise Price, Parimal Rana, Greg Rekas, Tracy Remain, Revol France, Shaun Richmond, Riegel, Robin Robertson, Deborah Ronnen, Meir Ronnen, Sheli Ronnen, the Rosenberg family, Jeri Rostron, Danita Ruiz, David Rutherford, Michal Ronnen Safdie and the Safdie family, Sheri Salata, Derek Sarno, Michelle Sass, the Scheidt family, Jacob Schiffman, Jesse Schiller, John Schoning, Guiseppi Scorella, Rosemary Serviss, Cheri Shankar, Paul Shapiro, Jeremy Shock, Steve Sidwell, Alicia Silverstone, Baxter Simmons, Damon Skweres, Elaine Sloan, Pier Smith, Laurel Spencer, Spike, Pat St. Clair, Bill Stewart, Susan Stockton, Kevin Stuart, the staff at Sublime: Lori, Jeremy, Stu, and the great crew; Chef Chris Thomas, Seth Tibbott, Lex Townes, Chef Eric Tucker (an inspiration to so many vegan chefs), Robert Tuschman, Sol Vaknin, Richard Vann, the staff at the VegiTerranean: Nick and the crew; Villeroy & Boch, Ray White, Bruce Wieland, Wayne Wiley, Oprah Winfrey, Paul Wong, Peter Wood, Jenny Woods, Megan Worman, Matt Wright, Mike Zarara, Lora Zarubin, and Mario Zehnder. ✻

PHOTOGRAPHY CREDITS

All photographs by Linda Long, except the following:

Pages 20-21, 24-25, 36-37, 48-49, 62-63, 98-99, 114-115, 152-153, and 188-189: Styling by Roscoe; photographs by Nathan Sayers

Page 10: © Victoria Pearson; page 79: Courtesy Tal Ronnen; p. 125: Courtesy Tal Ronnen; page 169: © Jenny Leche; Page 231 (1): © Sublime; (2): © Lisa Bailey; (3): © Melissa Kaseman; (4): © Ian Brandt; (5): © Kate Jacoby/Horizons Food of the Future, Inc.; (7): Courtesy Tal Ronnen; (8): © Mimi Giboin; (9): © Native Foods Café; (10): © Kate Mathis; (11): © The Veggie Grill; (12): © Flore; (13): © 2008 The Chicago Diner, Inc.

This book was produced by

 MELCHER MEDIA

124 West 13th Street
New York, NY 10011
www.melcher.com

Publisher: Charles Melcher
Associate Publisher: Bonnie Eldon
Editor in Chief: Duncan Bock

Executive Editor and Project Manager: Lia Ronnen
Associate Editor: Lauren Nathan
Production Director: Kurt Andrews
Production Assistant: Daniel del Valle